DIGITAL TRANSFORMATION OF MULTILEVEL TAX POLICIES AND ADMINISTRATION FOR RESILIENCE AND SUSTAINABLE GROWTH

Ehtisham Ahmad and Aekapol Chongvilaivan

OCTOBER 2024

ASIAN DEVELOPMENT BANK

6 ADB Avenue, Mandaluyong City, 1550 Metro Manila, Philippines
Tel +63 2 8632 4444; Fax +63 2 8636 2444
www.adb.org

ISBN 978-92-9270-923-5 (print); 978-92-9270-924-2 (PDF); 978-92-9270-925-9 (ebook)
Publication Stock No. TCS240468-2
DOI: http://dx.doi.org/10.22617/TCS240468-2

Notes:
In this publication, "฿" refers to Thai baht; "CNY" refers to Chinese yuan; "₹" refers to Indian rupees; and "$" refers to United States dollars, unless otherwise stated.
ADB recognizes "China" as the People's Republic of China.

Cover design by Cleone Baradas.

Contents

Tables, Figures, and Box

Tables

Figures

Box

Foreword

Domestic resource mobilization (DRM) is critical to achieving the Sustainable Development Goals (SDGs) and solving the climate crisis. As governments raise revenues to support these and other crucial development priorities, the rapid digital transformation of economies presents some risks as well as considerable opportunities.

This publication, *Digital Transformation of Tax Policies and Administration for Resilience and Sustainable Growth*, focuses on DRM policy options informed by evolving analytical approaches and experiences from federal, unitary, and small island states across Asia and Latin America. It is noteworthy that the analysis and recommendations apply across governance frameworks (federal or unitary) and continents.

A new tax policy framework, streamlined administration, and tighter information management will help to address rent seeking and base erosion and profit shifting. This can also provide a more effective approach to special economic zones for sustainable employment creation. Emphasis on local generation of information, national and international coordination, and financing also supports the SENDAI Framework to address pandemics and climate shocks. Moreover, local own-source revenues anchor access to private finance for climate-related mitigation and adaptation investments.

The digital transition must be linked to the broader policy goals of sustainable development. Revenue generation is key, but equally important are incentives for greater multi-level resilience, meeting the SDGs including climate-related objectives, foreign direct investment and employment generation, and enhanced equity. While using new technologies is part of this process, mere computerization of existing administrative arrangements, processes and procedures, is not sufficient.

There is much for the Asian Development Bank's (ADB's) developing member countries to learn from Latin American experiences. At the same time, our region is at the forefront of digital transformation. I believe this report will serve as a valuable reference for tax authorities, policymakers, researchers, and other stakeholders to better understand tax policy and administration issues and challenges, as well as policy options to address them. Along with support from the Asia Pacific Tax Hub, the insights from this report will also strengthen ADB assistance and operations to help developing member countries realize the potential of DRM as they build for a more prosperous, inclusive, resilient, and sustainable future.

Masatsugu Asakawa
President
Asian Development Bank

Acknowledgments

This study builds on joint work for the Philippines during 2023 that drew on a program on multilevel financing of sustainable development in developing countries coordinated by Ehtisham Ahmad at the London School of Economics (LSE). This study greatly benefited from views, insights, and suggestions of the experts and officials of the tax authorities at the Asia Pacific Tax Hub Distinguished Speaker Lecture on *Multilevel Tax Policy and Administration: South-South Perspectives on Digital Transformation* on 3 July 2024. The authors thank the Asia Pacific Tax Hub Secretariat and the Domestic Resource Mobilization Trust Fund for support. Donald Bobiash, Executive Director for Canada, Denmark, Finland, Ireland, the Netherlands, Norway, and Sweden; Justine Diokno-Sicat, Executive Director for Kazakhstan, Maldives, the Marshall Islands, Mongolia, Pakistan, the Philippines, and Timor-Leste; Ramesh Subramaniam, Director General and Group Chief, Sectors Group; Tariq Niazi, Senior Sector Director of Public Sector Management and Governance Sector Office; and Jose Antonio Tan, Director of Public Sector Management and Governance Sector Office, provided guidance and suggestions in preparation of this report. The authors would like to acknowledge coordination support by Sandeep Bhattacharya and Jayson Lopez, and excellent assistance by Ivy Laurente, Ma. Antoinette Figurasin, Lea Fenix-Cea, and Alaysa Escandor.

Abbreviations

AI	artificial intelligence
BEPS	base erosion and profit shifting
BIR	Bureau of Internal Revenue (Philippines)
BTB	business-to-business
CCCs	clean, compact, and connected cities
CCT	conditional cash transfer
CDMX	Mexico City
CIT	corporate income tax
DRM	domestic resource mobilization
ESI	estimated sustainable income
FBR	Federal Board of Revenue (Pakistan)
FDI	foreign direct investment
GBA	Greater Bay Area (PRC)
GDP	gross domestic product
GTS	Golden Tax System
IETU	*Impuesto Empresarial a Tasa Única*
IFI	international finance institution
IMF	International Monetary Fund
ISR	*Impuesto sobre renatas*
Lao PDR	Lao People's Democratic Republic
LGFV	local government financing vehicle
MDB	multilateral development bank
MSMEs	micro, small, and medium-sized enterprises
NAFTA	North American Free Trade Agreement
NIC	National Identity Card
NID	national ID
NPV	net present value
NTRC	National Taxation Reform Commission (Pakistan)
OECD	Organisation for Economic Co-operation and Development
PFM	public finance management
PISA	Programme for International Student Assessment (OECD)
PIT	personal income tax
PPP	public–private partnership
PRC	People's Republic of China
SDG	Sustainable Development Goal
SEZ	special economic zone
SIDS	small island developing states

STA	State Tax Administration (PRC)
SWF	sovereign wealth fund
TARP	tax and administration reform program
TaxRIS	Tax Revenue Information System in the Lao PDR
TIN	tax identifier number
TRD	Thailand Revenue Department
TSA	Treasury Single Account
UDIC	urban development investment corporation
UK	United Kingdom
US	United States
VAT	value-added tax

Executive Summary: Sustainable Tax and Multilevel Fiscal Reforms in the Digital Age

The G20 Finance Ministers' meeting in February 2024 also reiterated the importance of domestic resource mobilization as a critical element in enhanced resilience and financing sustainable growth, given that an increasing number of developing and emerging-market countries continue to face fiscal pressures, or debt sustainability challenges, in the aftermath of successive shocks, including the coronavirus disease (COVID-19) pandemic, climate disasters, and conflict affecting global value chains and public finances.

> "We at the IMF (International Monetary Fund)... together with the World Bank... have started a large domestic resource mobilization initiative, in which we will help our members comprehensively address how to increase resources in the public purse, how to use this money most effectively, how to give the financial sector confidence so that savings can turn into productive investment, and how to build capital markets to increase the efficiency and effectiveness of every penny." [1]

The Asian Development Bank (ADB) has engaged in these issues for several years—in many ways ahead of other multilateral development banks.

Asia covers the **full gamut of political systems, country size, and types of government:** (1) large federal states (India and Pakistan in South Asia); (2) large unitary states (the People's Republic of China [PRC] and Indonesia) as well as medium-sized countries (e.g., the Philippines, Thailand, and Viet Nam); and (3) small island states (from the very advanced like Singapore, to smaller and more fragile Timor-Leste and Kiribati). The paper focuses on **examples from each group, and also the important feature of learning across developing countries.**

We begin with a discussion of the similarities in the approaches to digital transitions and fiscal reform in Mexico and the PRC. Mexico is a federal state with elected governments at different levels of administration, and the PRC is a unitary state with appointed officials, but where the lower levels are perhaps more important than in Mexico. Similar instruments and strategies, including for digital transformations, have evolved across different regions and political systems—suggesting that strong lessons can be drawn from the selected case studies for a range of developing and emerging market economies.

1 IMF. 2024. IMF Managing Director Kristalina Georgieva's Statement at the Conclusion of the first Meeting of the G20 Finance Ministers and Central Bank Governors. *Press release.* No. 24/65.

Digital transformation involves efficient and timely management of information across different instruments and levels of government, and typically involves both policy and institutional changes. There have been ample examples of expensive computerization projects over the past couple of decades in many parts of the world. While computerization is an element of digital transformation, when applied to existing processes and procedures this just "pours concrete over the digital transformation agenda."

We examine how the combination of successive crises, and recognition of uncertainty[2] together with digital transformation possibilities in the presence of information asymmetries might lead to a new paradigm that affects the role of the state and governance, as well as institutions (Kuhn, 1970). A new approach would affect intergovernmental assignments regarding which level of government should be responsible for which function—especially regarding taxes, but also spending decisions (Ahmad and Brosio, forthcoming). Major problems are evident with policies and institutions based on static and steady-state models applied across regions based on assumptions of "market fundamentalism" (Tanzi, 2023).

The key objectives of tax reforms must include more than a revenue focus, and also be linked to a sustainable growth strategy aimed at reducing the cost of doing business and encouraging appropriate investment and employment generation, incorporating the effects on the environment, and addressing income distributional aspects. A multilevel focus is essential to address political economy constraints, ensure just transitions, and to facilitate access to private resources (local government bonds as well as public–private partnerships [PPPs]) to finance public infrastructure.

The effects of the tax system on **incentives (and ability) to cheat are hugely important**—and not just in developing and emerging-market countries. **Rapid digital transformation is shedding new light** on the "rent-seeking" issues as well as dealing more efficiently with the other policy objectives, including arms-length administration, national integration and distributional concerns, and "just" responses to climate challenges and increasing resilience.

Digital transformation of the tax system is closely linked with the agenda to address base erosion and profit shifting (BEPS). Both themes deal with limiting evasion, avoidance, and fraud. Governments are concerned with ensuring that the tax system collects revenues efficiently, without adversely affecting the cost of doing business and that foreign direct investment (FDI) is not discouraged. It is also important to complement and not hinder the digital transformation of the economy, such as the Indian Unified Payments Interface and Brazilian Pix (Carstens and Nilekani, 2024).

2 "Uncertainty" is defined as situations where the probability distribution of outcomes is not known, making it impossible to assign probabilities in any objective sense. Source: F. Knight. 1921. *Risk, Uncertainty and Profit.* Houghton Mifflin.

Structure of the Study

The study examines options for modernizing tax systems in the country types identified above; focuses on issues that are common across countries and political systems; and identifies those that are more country-specific (e.g., in relation to small island states, given their vulnerability to extreme shocks). To illustrate issues and reform options, we choose a country from each group identified to draw specific and more general lessons. Country experiences in Latin America have been taken very seriously in the tax and fiscal reforms in major Asian countries—even across political systems. The **cross-fertilization of policies across regions has been productive, especially the exchange of ideas between Asia and Latin America**. Many of the reform programs initiated in Mexico were picked up and developed in the PRC, and in some cases, lessons were learned in the reverse direction.

The similarity in policies, administrative arrangements, and reform options across differences in political systems and initial conditions is reassuring that the analysis and approach is soundly based. Most tax authorities have used value-added tax (VAT) to initiate reforms of policies and administrations, and the VAT remains the "tip of the spear" in the digital transformation from Mexico to the PRC, and to small island states like Singapore.

The study is structured as follows:

In Section II we examine some of the key issues that need to be reconsidered given climate and other shocks and digital transformation possibilities. These include overall targets for revenue generation in the medium term and measures to ensure fiscal sustainability without jeopardizing scope for investment and enhanced resilience, including at the crucial subnational level. Issues such as revamping special economic zones (SEZs), ensuring FDI while preventing corruption or base shifting (the BEPS agenda), and the political economy of the reforms are key issues to consider in a new architecture of rapid information generation and institutional simplification.

Section III juxtaposes the policy changes needed together with the streamlining of administrative arrangements, institutional arrangements, and simplification of processes and procedures. With the unification of information generation platforms, a key question is to maintain subnational autonomy and accountability, as well as access to private finance (bonds, PPPs, and loans). This can be ensured by permitting control over rate setting for assigned instruments.

Section IV draws on developing country experiences in meeting political economy constraints and in sequenced approaches to digital transformation in the PRC and Mexico, involving the policy framework, and changes in the tax administration and functions—especially the integration of key tax bases. Two very different large countries in Asia and Latin America are the focus in this section—Mexico has a federal constitution and "yardstick competition," and the PRC has a unitary constitution with appointed officials who are evaluated by different performance criteria. Yet, the issues faced, policy and institutional options, and the need to balance the interests of subnational jurisdictions have been common features in both types of systems. The remaining agenda to strengthen the local tier of government and own-source revenues is also remarkably similar.

Section V focuses on the issues arising in Asian countries, ranging from the federal countries in South Asia—India and Pakistan; **other unitary states** including the Philippines, Thailand, and the Lao People's Democratic Republic to illustrate the issues, **and contrasting small island states**—Singapore and Timor-Leste.

Section VI brings the arguments together with a unified approach to digital transformation that could guide policy options in ADB members. This focuses on the policy framework together with digital transformation of the tax and treasury institutions (the latter is important as part of ensuring the effectiveness of the revenue transformation, although not as fully covered as the revenue aspects). Maintaining local autonomy and strengthening the ability to respond to shocks to ensure the effective achievement of the Sustainable Development Goals (SDGs) and climate goals is critical in all contexts.

Key Takeaways

We illustrate the **general themes in designing and implementing a digital transformation of the fiscal system with a focus on domestic resource mobilization (DRM), and identify policies and institutional arrangements common across types of countries and political systems**. These will have a major bearing on the support provided by multilateral development banks for sustainable reforms in emerging market and developing countries. Such support has included expensive computerization and institutional reform programs in many ADB members. While spending and public finance management issues are not addressed explicitly, they are as important as DRM **for resilience and sustainable growth, and a coordinated strategy is essential in determining policy measures and their sequencing**.

- The political economy of tax reforms in multilevel countries ***requires adjustments in intergovernmental transfers and spending at different levels of government*** to offset gainers and losers across jurisdictions, regions, and types of households.

- A ***major premise of this study is that it is not appropriate to focus on specific taxes in isolation, or taxes and administration separately.***

- **Digital transformation depends on the seamless flow of information, and must involve both policy and institutional simplification in an environment with rapid technological advances.** Utilizing the potential of digital transformation involves simplification of processes and procedures, permitting policies to be implemented as they were designed to operate, without the constraints of semi-manual operating systems.

- **The introduction of a VAT or general sales tax (GST) has been used to modernize tax systems around the world since the 1980s,** but administrative constraints led to segmentation that reduced effectiveness of the measure. **Digital transformation in many countries is also spearheaded by reform to the VAT,** as seen in Mexico, the PRC, and Singapore.

    - Although VAT has been recommended by the International Monetary Fund as a revenue-earning instrument, a **segmented approach to administration in many countries has vitiated many of the other "structural" advantages**.

    - **Digital transformation with the VAT helps with achieving the structural benefits:**
        - **Effiiciency benefits and reducing the cost of doing business**—and if the full business-to-business (BTB) value chain is covered, permits immediate refunds on exports.
        - **Creating a unified economic space**—hugely important in many countries with diverse populations and centrifugal tendencies.
        - **Generating full information on wages and profits**—these are value-added components and hence provide information on the **more effective operation of the income and payroll taxes**.
        - **Reducing or eliminating possibilities of rent-seeking**—the information generated by the VAT applies also to SEZs and natural-resource sectors. It is important that production-sharing contracts or production in SEZs be subject to VAT, even if all the output is exported. This is because VAT generates information on quantities produced and exported, and eliminates possibilities of misrepresentation by private parties—hugely important in the petroleum sector.

- Digital transformation of VAT also facilitates **a new approach to SEZs** that permits sourcing from outside the SEZ, making more effective use of comparative advantages that a country has to offer.

- The **digitalized VAT would supplement the BEPS agenda**.

- **Full VAT facilitates FDI,** as seen in countries like Mexico.

- ***Administration.*** The logic of digital transformation highlights the importance of an **integrated tax administration that utilizes a national ID (NID) system for individuals, along with a consistent tax identifier number (TIN)**. This number would be the same as the NID for individuals and partnerships. This permits the exchange of information between and across taxes and cross-referring to information in other administrative agencies.

- ***Subnational autonomy*** is important in all systems, whether federal or unitary, especially since a large number of functions need to be implemented at the local level, and reflect local preferences and conditions. The **autonomy of junior jurisdictions is ensured by the ability to set rates at the margin**. **This autonomy is also necessary for sustainable access to private finance**—including subnational bond systems, direct borrowing, or PPPs, and is also needed to ensure **that "hard budget constraints" apply at the subnational level**.

    - **Rate setting at the margin is relatively straightforward** and can be handled with a single tax administration—the subnational jurisdiction just sets rates at the margin. A precondition for this option is assurance that the funds that are collected by an integrated national agency are immediately credited to the accounts of the relevant jurisdictions.

    - **Piggybacks on the income and carbon taxes** are relatively common and provide own-source revenues without the need for local administration. Such "surcharges" can also reflect local conditions, including income disparities, congestion, and pollution.

    - However, from a distributional perspective, piggybacked or surcharge arrangements would typically provide more resources to richer areas (where the affluent live and pollute with their cars and air-conditioning). It is important to consider introducing a **provincial- or state-level fiscal equalization** in multilevel countries to address distributional issues and labor market considerations. This is to offset migration of the youth to congested metropolitan areas, and address the increasing demographic challenges in many ADB members that pose significant medium-term risks.

- ***Simplified property tax system.*** One of the major constraints in the fiscal systems of emerging-market countries has been the failure to replicate the "textbook" ownership or valuation model of property taxes. The United Kingdom (UK) also abandoned this genre of property taxation for the recurrent property tax on noncommercial property—not only because it is difficult to establish ownership and market-based valuation, but also the political economy constraint of fixed-income households having to face substantial market-based tax changes. This is a serious constraint in most emerging-market countries.

- The solution to this political economy problem proposed by Alfred Marshall in the 1890s was to link the property tax on noncommercial properties to local service delivery. This solves the political economy problem; provides stable financing for the SDGs; and also helps with local accountability, including for access to private finance.

  - ***A recurrent property tax based on area-location-size*** is easy to implement with satellite-based mapping, together with low-tech verification of occupants.

  - ***For all property sales and commercial properties,*** the valuation basis remains because there is a robust market, and this can easily be locked in place with digital technology (e.g., Brazilian Pix) and blockchain developments.

- **Fiscal equalization is needed at the provincial or state level.** As with other forms of local taxation, there is an inequality bias in taxation—richer areas tend to generate more revenues and can exacerbate spatial imbalances. Thus, the local taxation agenda must be accompanied by an extension of fiscal equalization that is typically between the national and provincial or state governments, to be replicated at the provincial or state level.

- **Public finance management interface.** The digital tax framework must be accompanied by parallel developments in the payment and treasury framework so that subnational funds are deposited in their accounts in full and promptly.

These general considerations from the cross-country assessment **need to be examined in detail for specific countries, given that the state of digital infrastructure as well as the political economy and institutional constraints** differ from country to country.

Section I

Toward a Tax Reform Agenda for Sustainable Growth

Resilience, or ability to engage in support for pandemics or other shocks, depends on the strength of the domestic resource mobilization (DRM) underpinning—in terms of the ability to raise additional revenues, and financing additional liabilities, but also in generating sustainable growth. This is not simply a function of the level of general government tax-to-gross domestic product (tax/GDP) ratio, but also the effects on firms, households, the environment, and the political economy of gainers and losers among governments at different levels. Uncertainty and shocks lead to the need to reconsider both policies and administration—an additional factor in light of rapidly changing digital technologies.

There is propensity to rely on "rules of thumb" that are prevalent in policy advice emanating from many international agencies, and influence policymaking in many Asian countries. These are likely to be counterproductive (Rodrik, 2024)—misleading at best and wrong in many instances. Uncertainty cannot be addressed by policy choices based on ratings-like "box-ticking exercises" to guide tax and budget design, and numerical fiscal rules. Many of these issues have come to the fore in response to the coronavirus disease (COVID-19) pandemic, exacerbated by disruptions in global value chains and increasing frequency and intensity of climate shocks.

Numerical Targets for Tax-to-GDP Ratio and Debt

It is clear that countries with extremely low DRM at national and subnational levels will not have much fiscal space or access to finance. Consequently, such countries will have to be more parsimonious in supporting affected population groups. Contrasts between India and Pakistan are instructive (Table 1). India, with a tax/GDP ratio approaching 20%, was able to impose generalized lockdowns and run higher countercyclical deficits during the COVID-19 pandemic than Pakistan, which had a lower ratio of just over 10%. This is even though India has a higher general government debt level (approaching 90% in 2020 with very little prospect for significant reduction—see Eichengreen, Gupta, and Ahmed, 2023), in excess of the limit imposed under the fiscal responsibility legislation. Pakistan, with a debt-to-GDP (debt/GDP) ratio well below that of India, was bordering on debt

Table 1: COVID-19 Pandemic Emergency Responses in Selected Developing Countries Limited by Fiscal Space and Potential Debt Distress
(% of GDP)

	General Government Balance						Gross General Government Debt					
	2015	2018	2019	2020	2021	2022	2015	2018	2019	2020	2021	2022
Singapore	2.9	3.7	3.8	−6.8	1.2	0.4	102.2	109.5	127.8	149	147.7	134.2
Indonesia	−2.6	−1.8	−2.2	−6.1	−4.5	−2.3	27	30.4	30.6	39.7	41.1	39
India	−7.2	−6.4	−7.7	−12.9	−9.6	−9.6	69	70.4	75	88.5	84.7	83.1
Pakistan	−4.7	−5.7	−7.8	−7	−6	−7.8	57	64.8	77.5	79.6	73.6	75.8
Philippines	0.5	−1.5	−1.5	−5.5	−6.3	−5.2	39.6	37.1	37	51.6	57	57.5
Sri Lanka	−6.6	−5.1	−7.5	−12.1	−11.6	−10.4	76.3	83.6	82.6	93.7	102.2	117.7
Thailand	0.4	0.1	−0.8	−4.7	−7	−5.5	42.6	41.9	41.1	49.4	58.4	60.5
Bangladesh	−3.3	−4.1	−5.4	−4.6	−3.8	−3.8	28.2	29.6	32	34.5	35.5	39.1
Cameroon	−4.2	−2.4	−3.2	−3.2	−3	−1.8	31.1	38.3	41.6	44.9	48.6	46.4
Lao PDR	−5.6	−4.7	−3.3	−5.6	−1.3	−1.6	53.1	60.6	69.1	76	92.4	126.5
Ghana	−4	−6.8	−7.5	−17.4	−12.1	−9.9	53.9	62	58.3	72.3	79.6	88.8

COVID-19 = coronavirus disease, GDP = gross domestic product, Lao PDR = Lao People's Democratic Republic.
Source: IMF Fiscal Monitor, April 2023.

distress even prior to the pandemic, consequently, COVID-19 relief had to be carefully targeted by localities and sources of infection. However, the advanced digital national ID (NID) based support to selected communities limited the spread of the disease without the need for widespread lockdowns.

Numerical Fiscal Rules as a Proxy for Sustainability

While fiscal sustainability and strengthening DRM are important, there is nothing sacrosanct about a numerical debt limit of 60% of GDP,[3] or the International Monetary Fund (IMF) tax tipping point of 15% of GDP (Gaspar, Jaramillo, and Wingender, 2016). Singapore, with a tax/GDP ratio of under 15%, and a very efficient set of tax instruments and reserves, was able to ramp up the debt/GDP ratio to above 150% of GDP without adverse consequences on its ability to access private markets, or issues about resilience or medium-term sustainability. While Singapore does not have a numerical debt rule, its budget law prohibits borrowing for current spending. Consequently, all additional borrowing is linked to investment spending—in the form of a modified golden rule—"where borrowing is restricted to financing investments." In 2021, Parliament authorized issuance of bonds (around 20% of GDP) linked to financing strategic local infrastructure like tidal walls and "green" subway systems. This model of fiscal resilience can be contrasted with the much-praised fiscal consolidation

3 The Maastricht numerical targets were the result of a political compromise rather than an objective measure of sustainability, and are relaxed the moment there is a crisis—such as the recent COVID-19 pandemic. Proposals to revert to the Maastricht criteria are controversial.

in Jamaica that adopted a numerical fiscal rule. Major tax reforms and expenditure compression were needed to run primary surpluses of around 7% of GDP to bring down the debt/GDP ratio from 140% in 2012 to under 80% in 2023 (an escape clause permitted an increase in the debt/GDP ratio during the pandemic, above 100% of GDP in 2020).[4]

The key contrast between Singapore and Jamaica is that the **numerical fiscal rule in the latter prevents the investment in sustainable infrastructure needed to make the country more resilient** in the future given the increased likelihood of extreme events. But the Singapore-like modified golden rule requires tight monitoring of the investment operations, also to ensure that there is no leakage into current spending. The modified golden rule was adopted for Chinese local governments, but the distinction between current and capital spending was hard to enforce and monitor, especially in the absence of local own-source revenues. The spiraling debts of local government financing vehicles (LGFVs) pose a macroeconomic problem that cannot be handled at the local level. This was also the experience of Dubai World in 2009, and more recently in the bankruptcy of Woking Council in 2023.[5]

Countercyclical measures with weak domestic resource mobilization and problematic governance can exacerbate debt distress. A number of emerging-market countries are facing significant debt constraints following the COVID-19 pandemic and associated shocks, encapsulated in the recent World Bank Debt Report (2023).[6] In East Asia, in response to the pandemic, the Lao People's Democratic Republic (Lao PDR) ramped up countercyclical spending and consequently its debt/GDP ratio. The Lao PDR is now in serious debt distress given a weak DRM foundation.

The Philippines, with a tax/GDP ratio of around 15%, also engaged in countercyclical policies increasing its debt/GDP ratio by almost 20% of GDP during the pandemic, but has been careful about keeping it around 60% since then. The Philippine authorities limited the countercyclical measures to avoid repeating the painful experience of the debt restructuring of the 1990s, and also initiated a program to bolster DRM with ADB assistance (as described in section V2c).

4 S. Aslanalp, B. Eichengreen, and P.B. Henry. 2024. Sustained Debt Reduction: The Jamaica Exception. *Brookings Papers on Economic Activity*.

5 S. Kerr. 2020. Dubai World ends historic restructuring with final payment. *Financial Times*. 1 July. https://www.ft.com/content/e6338dd0-4d0f-4b85-821d-8e2406f365db.

6 As the World Bank's 2023 Debt Report shows, an increasing number of developing countries face significant risk of debt distress.

Base Erosion and Profit Shifting Agenda, Special Economic Zones, and Digitalization

The ability of multinational corporations and large high-tech companies to avoid paying tax has led to the Organisation for Economic Co-operation and Development (OECD)-coordinated effort on tackling **"base erosion and profit shifting" (BEPS)**. Enhanced global information generation and sharing are key elements of this initiative, and would benefit greatly from digital transformations.

Over the past decade or so, there have been **global efforts to prevent cross-border BEPS,** albeit with more progress on Pillar 2 on minimum global corporate taxation than on Pillar 1 dealing with fair taxation of digital services where they are consumed. Pillar 2 agreements will affect the design of investment incentives in tax systems including special economic zones (SEZs) as investing corporations would be liable to tax in their "home" jurisdictions if no tax is imposed in an emerging-market SEZ, negating the tax exemption carrot. Thus, foreign direct investment (FDI) will largely be driven by comparative advantages and agglomeration effects and will require strengthening and rationalization of the tax regime to make it more investment friendly.[7]

It is important to avoid transplanting tax or social protection policies from G7 countries—these often ignore the special characteristics of developing countries. For instance, copying Bismarckian social protection to Mexico resulted in "good intentions, bad outcomes" (Levy, 2008).

While a **fresh look at tax instruments and administration** is warranted, it is important to keep in mind the **wisdom regarding tax bases and levels of development** (Hinrichs, 1955; Tanzi, 1987). Thus, transplanting G7 policies and models to developing countries might not be appropriate. An example is the recent focus on **personal income tax (PIT)** in countries where the base is largely limited to withholdings from formal-sector wages, and turns the redistribution potential of the PIT into regressivity.[8]

Transplanting United States (US)-style ownership or valuation-based property taxes to developing and emerging-market countries has not been very successful. Despite a potential of 2%–3% of GDP, countries like India (which has operated such a tax for almost a century) and Mexico barely manage to generate 0.2% of GDP. This is inadequate to anchor the provision of the Sustainable Development Goals (SDGs) or provide an anchor for local governments to access private funds for financing infrastructure needed for sustainable growth.

7 See also the review by S. Beer, R.A. de Mooij, and L. Liu. 2018. International Corporate Tax Avoidance: A Review of Channels, Magnitude and Blind Spots. *IMF Working Paper* 19/158.

8 Despite the theoretical "progressivity" of the PIT, the practice is challenged in the US by the announcement by Warren Buffet that he has a lower marginal tax rate than his personal secretary—a point picked up by President Biden in his 2024 State of the Union Address calling for an overhaul of the Income Tax Code.

A corollary related to transplanting policies such as "land value capture," that work well, say in Japan, to developing countries like Pakistan, often translates to "land grab" by property tycoons. In the PRC, this policy without adequate preconditions has led to a huge off-budget local government debt trap and increasing spatial imbalances.

Welfare-Improving Directions of Tax Reform

As a starting point, policy options and reforms should focus on **"effective" rather than "nominal" taxes** (Ahmad and Stern, 1984, 1987, 1991).[9] This has major implications in designing just transitions to address climate challenges. While revenue objectives are important, **efficiency, distributional, and employment effects** must be included, as well as **externalities, such as the impact on the climate** (with consistency across tax and investment decisions). This does not imply that each tax instrument should meet all objectives, rather a combination of taxes and transfers, including incentive effects at different levels of government are needed (Ahmad and Brosio, 2006, 2015).

Welfare-enhancing directions of tax (and public sector pricing) reforms must include efficiency and distributional considerations, as well as externalities (e.g., for the environment). This could be based on the theory of reform (Drèze and Stern, 1987; Ahmad and Stern, 1991) that draws on the modern public finance and optimal tax literature. **Both tax and investment decisions need to be consistently addressed,** including the effects on firms, households in different circumstances, labor markets, and the environment. The political economy of reforms entails an assessment of the effects on different levels of government and the distribution of resources and responsibilities across them. First-generation federalism theory was based on US-centric market "normative" policies. However, actual outcomes did not conform to standard Musgrave-type models, giving rise to "second-generation" or "positive" practice and theory (Ahmad and Brosio, 2006, 2015).

Balancing gainers and losers across jurisdictions is especially critical in multilevel countries, and both policy and institutional design issues govern whether a reform works or not. Major reforms typically require offsetting sets of taxes and intergovernmental transfers to achieve "politically acceptable" outcomes to offset gainers and losers across governments at different levels.

9 E. Ahmad and N. Stern. 1984. The Theory of Reform and Indian Indirect Taxes. *Journal of Public Economics*. 23. pp. 259–298; E. Ahmad and N. Stern. 1987. Alternative sources of government revenue: illustrations from India. In D. Newbery and N. Stern, eds. The Theory of Taxation for Developing Countries. Oxford University Press for the World Bank; and E. Ahmad and N. Stern. 1991. Theory and Practice of Tax Reforms in Developing Countries. Cambridge University Press.

Recognition of shocks and digital transformation opportunities lead to a "third generation" of policy measures that depart significantly from accepted norms and institutions. The increasing frequency and severity of climate shocks, the recent pandemics, and conflict and potential disruption in global value chains highlight the importance of innovative digital solutions that are transforming the finance architecture in countries like the PRC and India, and also the public sector institutional and policy frameworks that either support or hinder the transformation.

Digital transformation of tax systems will involve the joint assessment of policy and institutional reforms, and cannot be achieved by computerizing existing policies and procedures—a common mistake, including by well-meaning international finance institutions (IFIs). There are great expectations concerning the use of digital technologies in generating revenues in an arms-length manner. However, partial approaches that digitize some processes and procedures with static models of tax administration, and without addressing policy reform options in some Asian countries, such as Pakistan and the Philippines, have not had much impact other than "pouring concrete on the digital transformation."

Tax and investment design affect growth potential. The design and operations of SEZs to "ring-fence" FDI from adverse domestic regulations and tax structure and cross-border interactions have been important in many Asian countries, as they were in the case of Mexico following the North American Free Trade Agreement (NAFTA) with the US in the early 1990s.

It is necessary to establish the enabling environment to take advantage of the BEPS agreement—particularly Pillar 2 that imposes a minimum global tax rate on corporations. This will require **a fresh approach to structural issues, including SEZs and streamlining the domestic enabling environment**. The Mexican experience following comprehensive tax reforms in 2013/14 is instructive, and many of the measures were also reflected in the Chinese reforms during 2015 and subsequently. In both countries, the full business-to-business (BTB) integration of the value-added tax (VAT) value chain enabled the establishment of broader linkages with the domestic economy. The creation of "high-tech zones" in the PRC, using the existing SEZs, like Shenzhen and areas of Guangzhou, enabled the creation of linkages within the Greater Bay Area (GBA). The completion of VAT reforms, and using digital tools to streamline institutions, policies, and procedures, facilitated linkages with the rest of the GBA. This has lessons for other Asian countries, and more generally.

A coordinated approach to policies, institutions, and processes and procedures, together with effective change management is required for the potential to be realized. A tax reform agenda to support resilient and sustainable growth should not only focus on revenues, while important, but also on the following:

- create incentives for *minimizing environmental damage*;
- generate *greater spatial equality* given disparities and centrifugal tendencies;
- lead to greater *local accountability*, especially for the SDGs, and form the basis for sustainable access to private finance; and
- utilize *technological transformations to ease the cost of doing business* while reducing incentives to evade taxes.

Political Economy of Multilevel Reforms

The political economy of reform requires a coordinated approach to offset gainers and losers, not just across firms and households, but also across governments at different levels of administration. Consequently, **fundamental change management is needed** that will involve taxes, intergovernmental transfers, and streamlined public finance management (PFM) systems, including treasury and payments networks, and new institutional arrangements to manage **completely new information flows**. **This will limit rent-seeking possibilities,** including by minimizing direct contacts between officials and taxpayers or recipients of benefits, especially transfers.

A more robust multilevel tax system, including at the local level, should be designed with appropriate weights given to human, social, and natural capital, and, of course, revenues. The broader focus is needed to anchor the SDGs for greater resilience to shocks. Local own-source revenues are also needed for accountability and to ensure sustainable local access to private capital to finance investments. Thus, the *tax system should provide signals to firms, workers, and households on decisions to invest, seek employment (including domestic and cross-border migration options), and patterns of consumption.* This would include taxation or public sector pricing of carbon-related activities and emissions at the national and local levels.

Coordinated actions at national and local levels will be needed to ensure financing for minimum service delivery levels across the country and achievement of SDGs, and for responding to shocks like the COVID-19 pandemic. These actions will influence incentives to migrate from lagging regions, and orderly policies for mitigation and adaptation in metropolitan areas. The creation of sustainable employment opportunities in clean, compact, and connected cities (CCCs) should also begin to address the huge problems with informality, especially in the crowded metropolitan slums.

Own-source sources of revenue at the local level are necessary to create greater "accountability" for the enhanced spending responsibilities, but do not require subnational administration. Accountability is not ensured with shared revenues and central government transfers, even if there is subnational administration. The poor performance of US-style ownership-valuation type property taxes in developing countries, including in Asia, poses significant constraints for devolution of responsibilities to local governments. In the Pakistan case, **greater devolution of resources under the 7th National Finance Commission award was designed to finance the SDGs** as well as disaster management. However, the failure of national and subnational DRM and a tax/GDP ratio that has been moribund at around 10% of GDP for almost 3 decades, and has resulted in unfunded mandates for the provinces and unsustainable fiscal deficits for the federal government.

Own-source revenues at the subnational level could also anchor sustainable access to private finance, including provincial or municipal bonds and public–private partnerships (PPPs), and attract private capital for infrastructure financing. In parallel, **there will be a need for tighter monitoring of uses of earmarked transfers and external assistance and ensuring envisaged outcomes.**[10] The use of PPPs, including at the subnational level, requires the liabilities to be recorded in the balance sheets at the appropriate level of government with associated provisioning (rules of the International Public Sector Accounting Standards governing the management of PPP liabilities).

10 Examination of the PFM or treasury options is beyond the scope of this paper.

Section II

Approaches to Tax Administration Reform and Digital Transformation

'Tax Administration is Tax Policy' or Vice Versa?

"Tax administration is tax policy" was a principle enunciated by Milka Casanegra de Jantscher, the head of the IMF's Tax Administration Division, in 1990.[11] Much of the advice from the Bretton Woods Institutions followed **the principle of adapting tax policies to facilitate tax administration in a largely manual or semi-computerized world**. Despite the warning by Bird and Casanegra de Jantscher (1992) that while it might be appropriate to begin to experiment with "modern techniques of information management in special large taxpayer units, by neglecting other taxpayers, revenue from all taxpayers may actually be lower."[12] The important finding that remains valid to this day is "that the more successful reforms did not merely involve computerizing antiquated processes but also the ***redesign and streamlining of processes and procedures.***"[13]

Unfortunately, practices in many developing countries, including Pakistan, have led to segmentation of tax bases, including for the VAT, and the increasing emphasis on large taxpayers, with lump-sum or presumptive taxation of small taxpayers. The pressures to keep raising the registration threshold (Keen and Mintz, 2004) resulted in **information breaks in the value-added chain reintroducing cascading and complexity besides encouraging rent-seeking behavior**. These discontinuities in information generation enhance both the incentives and ability to "cheat." The policy responses in the face of revenue shortfalls have been to rely on "gimmicks" and "quick fixes," ranging from lotteries and tax amnesties, and proliferation of withholdings that obfuscate and complicate the policy agenda.

Given restrictive trade policies and cumbersome legal and regulatory frameworks in many countries, there is a **tendency to encourage investment by providing tax holidays and exemptions**. **Using exemptions and special provisions for income distribution purposes, or to attract investment, are generally counterproductive**. This applies especially for VAT, where the break in the information chain on BTB transactions leads

11 M. Casanegra de Jantscher. 1990. Administering a VAT. In M. Gillis, et al., eds. *Value Added Taxation in Developing Countries*, World Bank. See also R. Bird and M. Casanegra de Jantscher, eds. 1992. *Improving Tax Administrations in Developing Countries*, IMF.

12 R. Bird and M. Casanegra de Jantscher, eds. 1992. *Improving Tax Administrations in Developing Countries*. IMF. p. 7.

13 Footnote 12, p. 9.

to cascading and makes it hard to provide refunds on exports. The VAT was devised with the objectives of removing cascading and encouraging exports and **creating a level playing field for investments and workers**. This can leverage FDI and domestic linkages, as well as reduce the cost of doing business. The VAT information from the full BTB value chain and digital transformation also **reduces the incentives of firms to "cheat" in their income taxes, and their ability to do so**.

Following the 1992 NAFTA, and the **creation of the "maquiladora" SEZs in Mexico, there was a proliferation of SEZs in emerging-market countries,** including the PRC. This was to encourage FDI by avoiding cumbersome tax and regulatory processes and procedures and also benefit from agglomeration effects. As shown below, especially in countries like Mexico and Pakistan, these **SEZs reinforced opportunities to evade taxes and encouraged all sorts of fraud,** including income tax, VAT, customs, and carousel (missing trader) fraud.

Tax policies and administration **need to align incentives facing different levels of government, firms, and households, and should remove possibilities of arbitrage or incentives to cheat**. The policies, however, need to be supported by an administration that generates information, probability of detection, and effective sanctions to block the ability to cheat. Modern tax administrations are typically organized on a functional basis that focuses on reducing the compliance costs for taxpayers, minimizing direct contacts between tax officials and taxpayers (except in the taxpayer services and facilitation department), and relying on information generation and audit to identify anomalies and stop cheating. Rather than the outdated model of rewarding officials who bring in more revenue, arms-length institutions prevent direct contact between tax officials and taxpayers to ensure that revenues are collected efficiently, and cash flows tracked to prevent rent-seeking and leakages.

A typical approach to subnational governance in many emerging-market economies, from Mexico to South Asia, **has been to establish separate tax administrations at different levels of government for split bases for the VAT and income taxes**. This leads to an increase in the complexity facing businesses. With VAT, there are possibilities of arbitrage and "cheating" as the integrated flow of information becomes harder to achieve. The overall quality of the administration, especially for wide-area taxes such as VAT and income tax, is then as good as the weakest link. The essence of local accountability, however, lies in the incentives that are generated by a control at the margin over rates and a specified base.[14] If a subnational government cannot control the marginal rate of a subnational tax, such as a partial VAT on services even with its own administration, the tax no longer represents own-source revenue but must be considered a shared revenue or transfer with relatively high collection costs as we see below.

[14] See F. Ambrisanio and M. Bordignon. 2015. Normative Versus Positive Theories of Revenue Assignments in Federations. In E. Ahmad and G. Brosio. 2015. *Handbook of Multilevel Finance*. Edward Elgar. There can be no hard budget constraints for subnational governments if they do not, at the margin, have control over the rates of a tax instrument that can be increased if the jurisdiction runs into difficulties in meeting its debt repayment obligations.

The typology of modern tax administration builds on a functional approach to administration that ensures arms-length operations (Figure 1) by ensuring **that no single administrator can influence a tax payment, and that there are checks and balances based on the generation of information, risk assessment, and audit**. The enforcement function is particularly important as it reflects the collection of information from various taxes into a common database—e.g., VAT, corporate income tax (CIT), and excises—that can be juxtaposed against real sector variables and third-party information (e.g., asset holdings and consumption patterns) that provide a basis to signal risk-based audit.

The outmoded approach to "incentivize" tax collectors, by assigning bonuses in relation to taxes generated, was needed in older systems of production-based excises (common in South Asia, for example) where the tax collector sat in a firm to monitor turnover. However, this was the source of great corruption and potential to "make deals" that are just not possible with the modern functional tax administration approach, and even more so with a fully digitalized and arms-length administration.

More recently, the emphasis from the IFIs has been on e-invoicing and electronic filing—key elements of a new digital platform. In Pakistan, there was no change in either the policy framework, particularly for small taxpayers and retailers who remained subject to lump-sum levies, or the institutional arrangements that might support a digitally based tax system. Consequently, the measures had no effect on the tax/GDP ratio revenue, which remains lower than in 1984.

There is a continuum between policies and administration that ensures accountability. Shared revenues do not ensure accountability (Figure 1), as they do not represent control over tax rates at the margin. Consequently, shared revenues cannot be used to anchor access to private finance, such as local government bonds, borrowing, and also provisioning for PPPs. In terms of incentives, shared revenues are like transfers (Figure 1, columns 1a and 1b). The fact that there is subnational administration does not affect this assessment. For instance, even if all elements of tax administration were carried out at the state or provincial level, but the rates at the margin were determined in common with all jurisdictions, as is being proposed in India (variant of 1b), the subnational jurisdictions cannot claim the revenues as own source. In some cases, the state or provincial government could use the tax administration to influence the tax base, but that generates distortions and a possible "race to the bottom."[15]

The control over rate structures is much more effective in generating accountability, even if all or some elements of tax administration are managed at a different level of administration. Indeed, face-to-face negotiations between taxpayers and the tax

15 In Mexico, the "race to the bottom" occurred with the vehicle tax assigned to the states in 2010, because of cross-border competition and the possibility of accessing "gap-filling" central transfers to meet deficits at the end of the budget year—see E. Piñeda, A. Ramirez, and A. Rastelett. 2015. A Mariachi Medley: Mexico's Long Road to Fiscal Federalism Reform. In V. Fretes Ciblis et al., eds. *Decentralizing Revenue in Latin America: Why and How?* Inter-American Development Bank.

Figure 1: Typology for Multilevel Taxes and Administration

Key Factors	Central Tax	1a	1b	2a	2b	3a	3b
		Shared Taxes		Own Revenue/Surcharge		Local Tax	
		Central Administration	Joint Administration	Joint Administration	Central Administration	Joint Administration	Local Administration
Rate/base	CG	CG	CG	CG	CG	LG	LG
Revenue	CG	CG/ LG	CG/ LG	LG	LG	LG	LG
Administration							
Registration	CG	CG	CG	CG	CG	LG	LG
Valuation	CG	CG	CG	CG	CG	LG	LG
Assessment	CG	CG	CG	CG	CG	LG	LG
Bill delivery	CG	CG	CG/LG	CG/LG	CG	LG	LG
Collection	CG	CG	CG	CG	CG	LG	LG
Enforcement	CG	CG	CG	CG	CG	LG	LG
Services	CG	CG	CG/LG	CG/LG	CG	LG	LG

Central Control → Local Autonomy

CG = central government, LG = local government.
Source: E. Ahmad. 2015. Institutions and Governance. In E. Ahmad and G. Brosio, eds. *Handbook of Multilevel Finance*. Edward Elgar.

administrator is a severe problem in the case of property tax (e.g., in South Asia as well as Mexico), reflecting the problems in many emerging-market economies. The issue of the property tax is discussed further in section VI.

By structuring the administration along functional lines, it becomes possible to concentrate on the key elements that make for an efficient tax structure. The flow and management of information is critical, both within a tax and across taxes. The registration function ensures that there is a common tax identifier number (TIN) for all taxes and levels of government—and facilitates the flow of information and linkages between different types of taxes, particularly VAT, income taxes, and payroll tax. The enforcement function depends on a central database and flow of information across different criteria, particularly for VAT and income taxes. This triggers flags for anomalies that need to be audited, with effective sanctions, as may be stipulated in the legislation. If the VAT and income tax bases are split, there is a danger that neither tax will perform effectively to raise revenues, while minimizing distortions and burdens on the taxpayers. With limited scope for local rate adjustments, there is even less justification to maintain or create multiple tax administrations, even though this tends to occur for political reasons, as in Pakistan following the 18th Amendment.

A local surcharge, generating the same amount of revenue as the revenue share, even with central administration, becomes an own-source of revenue if the subnational jurisdiction has the right to raise or lower the marginal rate that it has been assigned. The surcharge or "piggyback" is typically not recommended in the case of VAT, but could work well with an integrated base for PIT. Note that the income tax base is split in both India and Pakistan, with multiple administrations, creating significant loopholes and rent-seeking opportunities. The surcharge on the *full income tax* could facilitate the integration of the tax administration, without loss of own-source revenue-raising powers, and be a way to block the cheating for one of the fastest-growing revenue bases in emerging markets, as in India. Because the full tax base is used, the cheating in income taxes can be blocked with an appropriate use of information from the income tax—increasing the "total pie" available for the surcharge. Thus, higher revenues could be generated without a need to raise tax rates and further increase incentives to evade.

The surcharge approach is important in the context of a potential carbon tax that could form the basis for initiating structural changes, with the production and consumption patterns. Thus, the more congested and polluted metropolitan areas may require higher-than-standard carbon tax rates, without running the risk of the tax falling to zero in a race to the bottom (Ahmad and Stern, 2011). Again, the national tax administration capabilities would prevent the race to the bottom while providing rate-setting options for provinces or states and potentially also municipal governments.

Digital Transformations of Tax Administration and Policy

Digital transformations have become exponentially more important over the past quarter-century, but the preconditions for effective adoption are poorly understood. Often countries are tempted to purchase expensive IT systems without a clear idea of how to use this computing power, or what is needed in terms of revamping institutions, processes and procedures, or the policy framework.

Digitization of existing (semi-automated) processes and procedures is common. Unfortunately, this is like pouring concrete over the fiscal system and preventing the desired transformation.

Effective change management is needed and will entail a joint reconsideration of policies and institutions to maximize the advantages of digital transformation of the fiscal system.

A well-designed transformation completely changes the flow and timeliness of information. This will involve amending the associated organizational structures, and acquiring the skills needed for effective management of big data, and entails the crossing of information from various sources to wages and employment, assets and profits, as well as production and sales. This points to a need to triangulate information from various sources, in order to detect potential mismatches and inconsistencies. Also, with the use of blockchain for asset transactions, including those property related, there is instantaneous flow of information across agencies at the local and national levels. This results in a simplified set of functional requirements, and together with big data management, many of the labor-intensive operations of a typical administration become redundant. Maintaining multiple tax administrations is no longer necessary, and local autonomy is protected by rate setting as argued above.

The PRC and Mexico provide examples of the use of digital technologies together with policy reforms. The Mexican integration of the small taxpayer regime with VAT in 2014 was made possible by digital transformation, and had a huge impact on blocking ability to cheat in income taxes, and also helped create the preconditions for FDI *outside the maquiladora SEZs*. The Chinese digital and administrative reforms have gone furthest in this regard—with integration of VAT and the business taxes on services in 2015, it was possible to remove boundaries around SEZs, like Shenzhen, facilitating the creation of high-tech zones, such as the Greater Bay Area (GBA). All subnational tax administrations have been integrated into a single tax administration for all levels of government—reversing the arrangement that obtained before the reforms of the early 1990s, when the central government lacked a domestic tax administration and relied on revenues shared upward by local governments. More details are provided in the case studies below.

With digital transformations, the **administration for most taxes does not have to be local**. This arrangement applies to several policy options, such as piggybacks or surcharges on a national base, or use of blockchain for asset transactions that might be subject to taxation by more than one level of administration. **Local control can be established by setting rates at the margin, including on bands legislated by the center**. However, assigned subnational funds collected by a national tax administration must be promptly credited to the appropriate local treasury accounts—indicating that there needs to be coordination between tax and treasury reforms.

The coordinated flow of consistent information between the NID numbers and the TIN used by the tax administration is critical for **successful digital transformation**. This flow of information **is central for the digital transformation of tax policies and rationalizing fiscal institutions,** including the tax administration and treasury functions and institutions.

Digital transformations create significant new options for reforming DRM. These depend on **timely and accurate information generation** that facilitates tax-on-tax interactions and potential to change both policies and supporting institutions. **Changes in the policy framework** are an essential component in a digital transformation. This is seen in the resistance to adoption of point-of-sales measures by small businesses subject to lump-sum taxation in the case of Pakistan and the Philippines, as the tax policy regimes did not change. **Changes in institutional design** are also needed, e.g., with the use of **artificial intelligence (AI) and big data**. A very different structure of a national tax administration for all taxes emerges, as seen in the case of the PRC.

Section III

Political Economy of Tax Reforms—Learning from Developing Countries

Major tax reforms are seldom feasible without incorporating the ramifications of tax-on-tax interactions, and the need to offset gainers and losers not just across firms and households, but also across jurisdictions at different levels of government. This section highlights the experiences of two major emerging-market countries—Mexico and the PRC. It highlights how they dealt with both political economy and administrative challenges.

Why Compare the People's Republic of China and Mexico?

Although unitary PRC and federal Mexico have very different political systems, and Mexico was certainly more developed in the early 1980s, they are **large multilevel countries that have undertaken far-reaching fiscal reforms and adopted very similar policies and institutional tools over time**. The PRC has typically adopted policies and institutions after Mexico, and in most cases has improved on both design and implementation, and has become the second-largest economy in the world. However, there has been some exchange of knowledge in the reverse direction. Both face similar challenges in the future to bolster their fiscal systems. The robustness of policies across political systems and continents provides some assurance about the more general applicability of their shared experiences and challenges.

It is worth keeping in mind that the **initiation of major reforms in both the PRC and Mexico in the early 1980s was not for revenue enhancement purposes, but to reduce production disincentives and distortions, especially at the subnational level**. Remember that at this stage, Mexico had a reasonably well-developed tax administration at the federal level—the PRC did not and relied exclusively on local tax administrations and upward revenue sharing. At this stage, the PRC had a tax/GDP ratio of almost 30% of GDP, and Mexico had abundant oil revenues.

Why Do Firms Cheat? Evidence from Mexico

Mexico 1980s Reform to NAFTA

Mexico in the late 1970s relied on a federal turnover tax, numerous excises, and a plethora of distortive state (subnational) taxes. The turnover tax (recommended by some experts for developing countries as a third-best option)[16] encouraged vertical integration, hence large firms, made it impossible to determine what refunds to give to exporters, discouraged agriculture, and taxed investments. A VAT was introduced to "streamline indirect taxation and to reenforce taxpayer compliance. More than 30 federal excise taxes and 300 state taxes were eliminated when VAT was introduced" (Gil Diaz, 1987, p. 345). The fact that the ***VAT applies to imports, but the tax element in the price of exports is credited or refunded, made the tax system efficient for investors and it was much harder to evade taxes***. This is an important lesson that is reinforced by the latest tax reform discussed below.

The political economy of the Mexican tax reform was facilitated by a revenue-sharing formula with the states—the *Participaciones* (the federal Participation Fund)—largely on an origin basis. This introduced an intergovernmental problem reflected in other countries, like Pakistan, that share national revenues: both the size of the pie to be redistributed and the spatial distribution implies that "somebody's gain is someone else's loss." The revenue neutral rate was estimated at 13% but political negotiations in an inflationary environment reduced it to 10%. However, the overall tax level was maintained as the VAT led to a sharp increase in CIT collections, "reflecting the better compliance generated by the mechanics of VAT" (Gil Diaz, 1987, p. 346).

Despite the enhancements in the tax system, **the overall regulatory and trade regimes remained fairly restrictive**. The NAFTA was designed to enable a better integration of the North American economies. The maquiladora regime (SEZ) along Mexico's northern border with the US, was designed to enable US corporations to take advantage of Mexico's cheap labor without having them cross into the US. The SEZ with exemptions from customs, VAT, or income taxes introduced an "exemption" culture that permeated the rest of the tax system in Mexico. The SEZ principle was copied in the PRC and throughout Asia.

Since Mexico introduced VAT in the early 1980s, successive governments have provided additional incentives for investment and production by reducing rates in sensitive or "border regions," along with exemptions and domestic zero rating for both investment and distributional objectives. The base for the major taxes (including both VAT and income taxes) was split, with the allocation of

[16] A. Brockmeyer et al. 2015. Production versus Revenue Efficiency with Limited Tax Capacity: Theory and Evidence from Pakistan. *Journal of Political Economy*. 123 (6). pp. 1311–1355.

the small taxpayer regime (called REPECOS) to the state level. With access to "gap-filling" transfers from the federal government to meet state deficits, there was no incentive for the latter to pursue the "hard-to-tax" groups under the REPECOS, and the Mexican Tax Administration (SAT) estimated that there was 95% evasion under the system. The "gap-filling" transfers also had a negative impact on incentives to implement own-source revenues, such as the piggyback on the income tax that has been an option, or the vehicle tax, *tenencía*, after it was fully devolved to the states in 2010. The net result was that the non-oil tax/GDP ratio for general government was around 10%. The C-efficiency[17] of the Mexican VAT was similar to that in Pakistan, at around 25%, among the lowest in the world.[18] Consequently, an "inefficient" VAT could not be a replacement for the distorting payroll tax.

The Mexican income tax, *Impuesto sobre renatas* (ISR), also suffered from growing base erosion. Many of the beneficiaries were large firms with important political connections. Once given, the special provisions and tax breaks become virtually impossible to remove—a phenomenon common also in other emerging countries (and in developed countries for that matter). Initially the Mexican government tried to rectify this with a "minimum tax," called the minimum asset tax (called IMPAC), a form of gross asset tax widely used in Latin America. As with the ISR, this minimum asset tax was aimed at the largest taxpayers, who also have a greater ability to engage in tax avoidance. Nevertheless, the influence of vested interests proved too strong; the government was unable to overcome the opposition in the Senate to address the holes in either the income tax, ISR, or VAT.

Levy (2008)[19] argued that inappropriately designed social protection systems can raise the cost of doing business and increase the incentives for firms to "hide" outlays on labor, and for workers to accept temporary and informal contracts (footnote 17). Both of these incentives lead to inefficient outcomes and reduce potential growth—constituting "good intentions but bad outcomes." The recommendation was a shift from the high payroll tax on firms that adds to the cost of doing business, to the VAT that should be neutral to production and exports. However, the Mexican VAT was not capable of performing this function, and the "good intentions, bad outcomes" story applies to the Mexican tax system, particularly the VAT, as much as to the financing of the social security system. The use of the payroll tax to finance local government administrative expenses is perhaps more pernicious than financing social benefits.

17 The C-efficiency of the VAT is simply the ratio of VAT revenues to consumption divided by the standard rate. The most efficient VATs range above 90%.

18 A. Antón, F. Hernández, and S. Levy. 2013. *The End of Informality in Mexico? Fiscal Reform for Universal Social Insurance*. Inter-American Development Bank.

19 See also A. Antón, F. Hernández, and S. Levy. 2013. *The End of Informality in Mexico? Fiscal Reform for Universal Social Insurance*. Inter-American Development Bank.

There are two mechanisms for firms to evade or avoid taxes. The first involves firms avoiding coming into the VAT or ISR net by remaining below the annual turnover threshold, or splitting into different firms to avoid paying tax. This is the typical case discussed in the literature and formalized in Keen and Mintz (2004). The revenue losses from this reconstitution by "avoiders" at lower levels of turnover are likely to be small, and this provides the logic for the strong support from the international agencies to raise the registration threshold to "reduce the burdens on the tax administration" (see, for example, the report by the IMF and World Bank to the G20) (footnote 1). Small traders and small and medium-sized enterprises (SMEs) exercise enormous political power in countries such as Pakistan, and are a stumbling block to meaningful reforms—unless they can be persuaded simultaneously that the losses will be offset by rationalization of the income taxes, as in Singapore. However, this also requires the establishment of an arms-length tax administration that does not impose additional costs of doing business, especially on small firms.

While there is some evidence for the Keen and Mintz (2004) hypothesis in Mexico, **the second and by far the more important cheating mechanism is outright evasion by larger firms,** which also have much greater political clout than the smaller traders in a more advanced country like Mexico (Ahmad, 2021).

There are two principal channels for rent seeking:

(i) ***Generating incentives to cheat through pricing discontinuities and arbitrage,*** including multiple VAT rates for the same good with special regimes for border regions and the maquiladoras (SEZs), together with holes in the direct taxes, and high marginal rates that add to the cost of doing business. Rents are generated due to multiple pricing regimes, SEZs, exemptions, tax preferences, and domestic zero rating.

(ii) ***Absence of information on transactions or components of value added.*** These generate silos of tax information within tax groups and across tax instruments. Breaks in the value-added chain, and presumptive mechanisms to estimate VAT liability used extensively—for example, in the Pakistan case—prevent the self-policing aspects of the VAT from operating. This is exacerbated by the weak or ineffective tax administrations for components of the tax system—which, in the Mexican case, was the small taxpayer regime that opened the floodgates of informality.

The overall incentives to cheat in Mexico are summarized in Figure 2. Larger firms are higher up in the picture and are represented by larger rectangles. Similarly, more compliant firms are on the right of the picture and the degree of compliance is depicted by a greater extent of shading of the rectangle.

Several cases can be identified:

- *REPECOS and adjusters.* Firms with turnovers below Mex$2 million could join the REPECOS regime for small businesses (the white boxes to the bottom left in the chart). Very few of these pay any tax in Mexico. Although there is no legal registration threshold for the VAT, this became the de facto threshold. This group of smaller taxpayers is effectively written off by IFIs, but includes the "adjusters," who legally reduce turnover to stay under the REPECOS threshold.
- *Enanos or ghosts.* In Mexico, there are many so-called "enanos," too large to be eligible for REPECOS, but pretending to be eligible regardless. Further, since enforcement of REPECOS is generally very weak, businesses know that if they pay something, they will keep the state government happy and keep SAT off their backs. These are the "ghosts" identified by Kanbur and Keen (2015).

Figure 2: Incentives to Cheat in Mexico

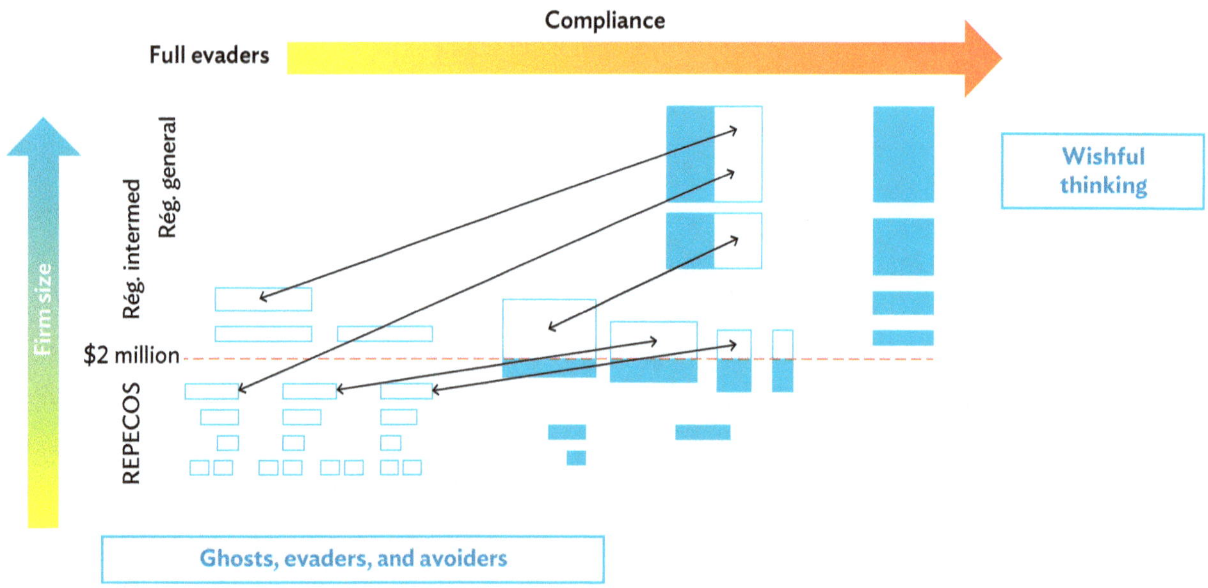

Note: Rectangles represent firms, and rectangle size represents the size of the firm. Rég. general = regular tax regime applying to large taxpayers; Rég. intermed = tax regime for intermediate-size taxpayers; REPECOS (Regimen de Pequeños Contribuyentes) = small firms subject to administration by the states. Academics and some international agencies think of large taxpayers as compliant and honest, which is wishful thinking.

Source: E. Ahmad 2021. National and Subnational Tax Reforms to Address Informality. In C. Deléchat and L. Medina, eds. *The Global Informal Workforce*. International Monetary Fund.

- *Larger firms.* As argued by Levy (2008), there is a great deal of cheating by middle- and large-sized firms that hide transactions, turnover, employment, and profits by trading with enanos, truly REPECOS firms, ghosts, and other cheaters. These firms reduce payroll and profits taxes and avoid the VAT chain altogether.

- *Honest firms.* Some firms may not be able to cheat—international agencies believe—either because they are run by multinationals, or are too large to do so in an undetected manner. However, the large firms are often reflective of the best-connected "vested interests" and multinationals are better able to avoid taxation than most of the large domestic firms, for example, by moving corporate headquarters to low-tax jurisdictions such as Ireland, Luxembourg, Panama, or the Bahamas. We have added this "honest" firm categorization to those in Figure 2 for the sake of completeness.

All the possible forms of VAT fraud are greatly facilitated by the existence of the maquiladora regime and particularly by its lack of transparency, which allows firms to hide or disguise activities and the ever-widening definition of a maquiladora, which allows increasing numbers of firms to enter the regime.

The revenue sinkholes created by the interaction between the maquiladoras regime and the VAT are summarized in Figure 3. The orange, dotted arrows depict a standard carousel fraud. Businesses that import inputs can pass on the input credits to other Mexican firms, which in turn can export and claim the input credits. This kind of fraud is greatly facilitated by the ability of maquiladoras to operate as part of a larger group of firms both within Mexico and abroad and with very few reporting requirements to the Mexican authorities.

The green, dashed arrows depict a more straightforward export fraud in which a pair of related firms, one maquiladora and one outside the regime, collude to claim an input credit for a transaction that never occurred. Finally, the red, solid arrows show the most pernicious fraud. Under the maquiladora regime, bonded imports are permitted without incurring a VAT liability, provided the transformed outputs are re-exported. These inputs or their resulting transformed outputs are then passed on to another Mexican company, which then sells them in the domestic market without ever having paid the VAT on the imported inputs. Customs data show that only an estimated 50%–60% of the inputs imported under this scheme ever actually leave the country.

Empirical assessments of tax and economic census data provide support for the Levy hypothesis, but show that there are both the incentives and ability to cheat in firms of **all** sizes. The smaller- and middle-sized firms do not appear to have a monopoly on cheating the tax administration. Under the circumstances, there are unlikely to be many firms that would not take advantage of the opportunities to maximize profits. To expect that **raising the VAT registration threshold per se would raise revenues would be wishful thinking indeed**.

Figure 3: The Maquiladora Sinkholes

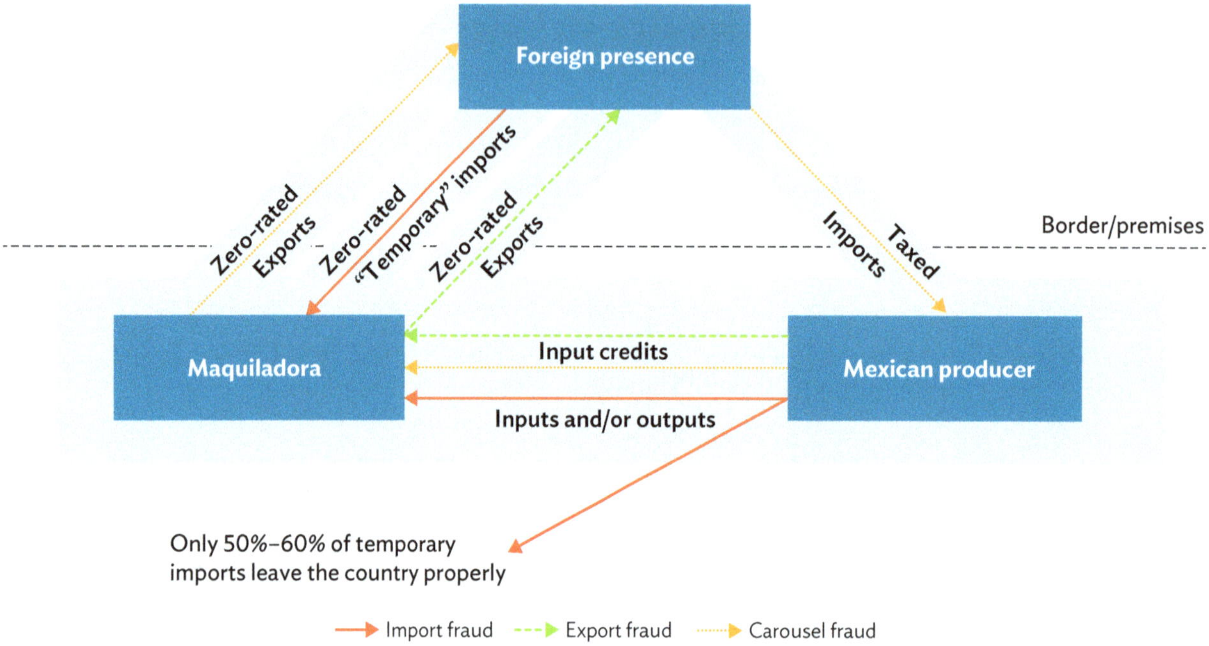

Source: E. Ahmad 2021. National and Subnational Tax Reforms to Address Informality. In C. Deléchat and L. Medina, eds. *The Global Informal Workforce*. International Monetary Fund.

People's Republic of China—Building on Mexican Initiatives

Deng Xiaoping's Responsibility System 1980s to 1993/94 Reform

The Chinese case is of **special interest because of the close links between tax and structural reforms** (Ahmad et al., 2013). While 100% profits taxation of firms and farms raised over 25% of GDP in revenues, collected by local tax administrations (the PRC did not have a central tax administration other than for customs at this time) and 50% shared upward with Beijing, the system was damaging to initiative. Deng Xiaoping in the late 1970s with the Responsibility System began to create an incentive system to encourage enterprise and investments, reducing the tax rate, but administration remained at the local level. A key focus was on coastal "hubs" to generate employment opportunities. The effective reduction in tax rates permitted local governments and enterprises to use retained funds for investment and growth (Shi, 1995).

Both the total revenues generated, as well as the proportion shared upward with the central government, fell precipitously. While there was a positive impact on producers, the declining overall revenue generation had a negative impact on public finances—with the total tax/GDP ratio falling from 25% at the start of the reforms to around 10% by 1992/93 (Figure 4).

The fall in total revenue collection affected the incentives of local governments to share revenue upward. Consequently, the central government's share of total revenues also fell precipitously, despite various attempts to incentivize local officials (Gao, 1995). The central share, which had been around 55% of total revenues at the start of the Responsibility System reform, fell to well under 30% by 1993 (Figure 2), as local governments sought to protect local interests in the face of falling revenue collections.

Consequently, in the absence of modern fiscal institutions and instruments, the structural changes generated a fiscal crisis. Thus, by 1992/93, the plummeting tax/GDP ratio, as well as the decline in the share going to the center, meant that the central government's ability to maintain macroeconomic stability, ensure redistribution, or meet the fundamental responsibilities of a nation state was seriously compromised.

Figure 4: Evolution of Tax-to-GDP Ratios and Central–Local Shares in the People's Republic of China

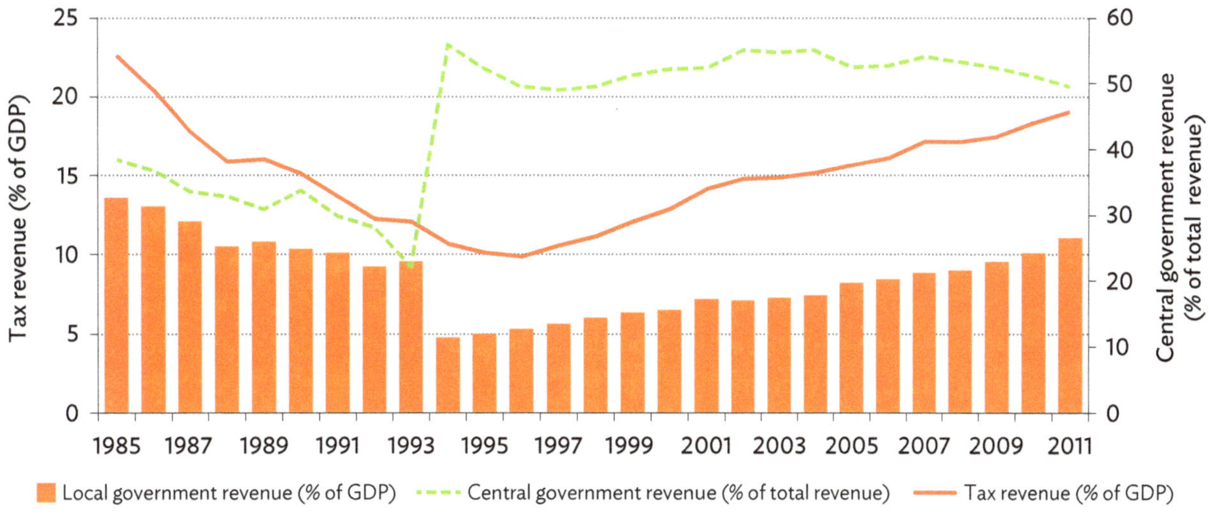

GDP = gross domestic product.
Source: E. Ahmad. 2018. Rebalancing in China: Fiscal Policies for Sustainable Growth. *Singapore Economic Review*. 63. pp. 861–884.

By 1993/94, a major tax reform was needed to consolidate the structural reforms made because of the Responsibility System, and strengthen the ability of the central government to maintain macroeconomic stability and public investment (Ahmad, 2008; Ahmad, Rydge, and Stern, 2013).

The establishment of the State Administration of Taxation (SAT) on the most modern lines, and central revenue-raising powers, facilitated the introduction of an "investment-type VAT." Despite advice from the IFIs to the contrary, SAT officials decided to begin to match VAT invoices, and initiated Phase I of **the "Golden Tax System" (GTS) to develop a computerized and centralized VAT system, initially focusing on invoice matching**.

As in Mexico, the **political economy of the Chinese tax reform had to offset opposition from provinces, and a system of transfers formed part of a "package" of tax administration and policy reforms,** designed to minimize losses and share benefits across rich and poor provinces alike. This significantly improved on the Mexican 1980s reform package. Key elements of the package included the following:

- prevention of losses among local governments by a **"hold harmless" clause**—this guaranteed all provinces 1993 levels of revenues in absolute terms in perpetuity;
- **providing a share of the (increasing) revenues from the VAT** with the provinces that generated the value added—these were mainly the richer ones;
- **introducing a modern "equalization framework"**—this enabled all provinces to provide similar levels of services at similar levels of effort. The version adopted in the PRC was based on the Australian model, but with simpler factors, and ensured a "buy-in" from the poorer provinces; and
- **the most innovative measure in the "package" provided for a revenue-returned policy** to provide additional funds to the better-connected provinces, but on a gradually decreasing basis. This measure was critical in providing for a concentration of resources in existing "production hubs," largely along the coast, making use of the existing connectivity in the short run to generate investment, exports, and employment opportunities.

The **VAT initially implemented in 1994 was applied only to manufacturing,** largely because of administrative constraints, and because of the need to leave at least some tax handles in the hands of provinces (this was the local business tax mainly on services). Further, the VAT was of "investment type"—i.e., that VAT on capital purchases could not be offset against VAT on sales. This again was to meet the revenue targets of the government and was simpler to administer with the nascent SAT. Almost 15 years later, in the aftermath of the 2008 global economic crisis, there was pressure to reduce the cost of doing business and protect Chinese competitiveness, and besides the tax/GDP ratio had almost doubled since the early 1990s. **The investment-type VAT was converted to a consumption-type VAT**, with VAT on capital purchases permitted to be offset against VAT on sales.

Phase II of the GTS built on the successes of Phase I, including other taxes besides the VAT, and facilitated data sharing across taxes and regions, and improved taxpayer services and compliance.

Computerization Is Necessary but Not Sufficient

In Mexico, during the decade following the NAFTA, **there were several attempts to reform the VAT and income taxes in isolation, and none were successful**. Despite the modernization of SAT, with a **new computer system developed** in the early 2000s, there was no appreciable impact on the non-oil revenues, which continued to stagnate near the 10% of GDP level—similar to that in Pakistan. The C-efficiency of the Mexican VAT was also similar to that of Pakistan, and for similar reasons—the tax did not cover the value chain appropriately.

To "plug" the seeping holes in the tax, the government introduced in 2007 another form of minimum tax, creditable against the ISR (CIT) through the *Impuesto Empresarial a Tasa Única* (IETU). This adopted the VAT principle even though it was a minimum income tax. The reform addressed political economy concerns through a Chinese-style "stop-loss provision" and a rationalization of intergovernmental transfers. This ensured that no state lost revenues because of the reforms (Ahmad et al., 2007). This "reform package" was approved by Congress, presaging the deeper reforms to follow in 2013.

While the IETU had some disincentive effects, the underlying value-added design did not disadvantage investments as much as a turnover tax would have. However, the IETU added to the complexity and burden of tax compliance. Not surprisingly, its base began to display additional breaks at the behest of powerful interests that had plagued the ISR in the first place. While an additional 0.4% of GDP per annum was generated after 2007, this was insufficient "plugging of holes." Moreover, IETU did not significantly expand the base of non-filers. Further consolidation of the income tax base was required to build upon gains and generate information. A simple and full-base VAT was still needed to identify non-filers, and reduce incentives to cheat, together with a credible audit threat. However, if this were feasible in the first place, the IETU would not have been needed.

It is noteworthy that another attempt to close the holes in VAT failed in 2010. This would have provided compensatory benefits to households through the *Oportunidades* scheme—the famous conditional cash transfer (CCT) on which many other schemes, including many in Asia, are modeled. First, many of the "losers" from a VAT reform are urban households and the CCT provides benefits mainly to poor rural households, making it an inappropriate compensation mechanism for many energy price and tax reforms. Second, the main losers in a VAT reform tend to be firms with vested interests, and possibly some states, given the revenue-sharing system. The interactions between the "holes" in the VAT and the special provisions in the ISR present a formidable incentive to cheat and engage in informal activities, but which cannot be addressed by the CCTs,[20] as seen in Mexico in 2010.

Next-Generation Tax Reforms—Policy, Administration, and Digital Transformation

Despite spectacular successes with tax reforms in the PRC since 1993/94, and partially in Mexico in 2007, a **number of significant problems remained, especially concerning distortions and disincentives—reflecting current issues in many Asian countries**. Split bases, especially for the VAT, led to higher costs in the PRC that began to affect competitive positions as the yuan strengthened in global markets, and the global economy was affected by the 2008–2010 financial crisis. In Mexico, the split bases led to incentives to cheat and evade—affecting the ability to raise revenues and attract FDI beyond the maquiladora SEZ zone. As we will see in this section, a combination of policy reforms, directed to consolidating resilience and efficiency, made use of developments in digital tools, together with a willingness to restructure administrations, and made it possible to carry out further and far-reaching reforms in both countries.

This section first describes the reforms in Mexico, initiated by the outgoing Calderón administration in 2012, but implemented very effectively in 2013/14. In 2016, in the PRC, facilitated by the enhancements to the GTS, all **local business taxes were merged with the VAT** in 2016, and all local tax administrations were integrated with the central State Taxation Administration in 2018. **The reform was designed to reduce the cost of doing business and laid the foundations for a new approach to SEZs,** and especially the creation of high-tech zones. This reform also anchored the proposed rebalancing in the 14th Five Year Plan from congested and polluted coastal metropolises to clean, compact, and connected cities (CCCs) in the interior. This should be environmentally attractive, support a core of Chinese commitments for reduction in emissions, and also help to reduce the reliance on exports with a shift to domestic consumption, especially in the interior (Ahmad et al., 2021).

20 Of course, there are other problems with CCTs that have become apparent in Mexico that are relevant for other emerging-market or developing countries including Indonesia and Nigeria that are considering both tax reforms (such as the carbon tax) and energy price adjustments. The "reformed" *Oportunidades* program was abolished by the AMLO administration in 2020.

In both the PRC and Mexico, the latest stage of tax reforms involved policy measures, digitization, and restructuring the tax system, and was initiated by "fixing" the VAT.

The Mexican 2013/14 Tax Reforms

Toward the end of the Calderón administration in 2012, it had become clear that **political economy constraints prevented the reform of a single tax in isolation—especially the VAT**. Given the volatility of oil prices and the realization that Mexico's petroleum reserves were rapidly depleting, the administration initiated a full review of the main constraints and potential directions of reform to provide inputs for the following administration. Mexico reverted to a "package" approach, reminiscent of the PRC in 1993/94, and prepared a set of major adjustments to federal taxes that offset gainers and losers among states. Poor people were protected by maintaining the VAT exemption for nonprocessed foods and medicines, and with the introduction of a universal (noncontributory) pension for those aged 65, as *Oportunidades* was transformed into a lump-sum grant for training or starting businesses.

The core of the reform **was again driven by the changes to the VAT, with the effective integration of the REPECOS regime, facilitated by digital coverage of the full value-chain**. The new Regimén Integrado Federativa regime for small taxpayers was designed around free accounting packages provided to small taxpayers that computed liabilities for all taxes, but more importantly issued electronic invoices for business-to-business (BTB) transactions. If the electronic system were not used, purchasers would not be able to claim input tax credits, and would effectively be treated as final consumers. The tax/GDP ratio increased by 4 percentage points within 4 years, and also put Mexico in a more robust position to face the shocks that were to come in the form of the global value chain disruptions and the COVID-19 pandemic. Indeed, the transformation of retailers and small taxpayers made it easier for Mexican suppliers to interface with US firms like Walmart during the pandemic, leading its chief financial officer to recommend this measure to all their supplying countries.

A **structural consequence of the Mexican reforms involving the completion of the VAT chain is that the whole country becomes a free trade zone**, not just the maquiladora areas. If taxes on inputs sourced from any part of the country can be credited on exports, location decisions can be made on the basis of connectivity, skills availability, public services, and quality of life. Figure 5 shows some of the major investments in the auto sector that have taken place since the 2013/14 reforms. Mexico is one of the main countries that have benefited from the disruptions in global value chains and "nearshoring" and has replaced the PRC as the largest trading partner of the US.

Figure 5: The 2013 Fiscal Reforms Turned All of Mexico into a Free Trade Zone

Car plants in Mexico

- Walmart CFO praised the small taxpayer e-invoicing system for integration of value chains during pandemic.
- Major new investment by BMW for EVs ($1 billion+) in San Luis Potosi
- Mexico is the only LAC country to have benefitted from "nearshoring" and value chain disruptions.

CFO = chief financial officer, EVs = electric vehicles, GM = General Motors, LAC = Latin America and the Caribbean, VW = Volkswagen.
Source: E. Ahmad and H. Viscarra. 2021. in LSE Program on Financing Sustainable Transition in China and Mexico.

A significant constraint in Mexico is the **absence of a unique national identifier number for individuals**. This will be needed for any significant improvements in the PIT regime, building on the solid foundation of the integrated VAT that has been established.

One of the **main problems with the market-based reform, also reflected in the PRC, is that activities and workers gravitate to the more developed metropolitan areas**, and this causes considerable disparities. Further, the national tax reforms leave the states and local governments with few own-source tax handles, and this makes it difficult for lagging regions to generate the investments needed in infrastructure and public services needed to attract firms and workers. It is also harder to access private financing or establish sustainable local government bond systems, locking the lagging states into a low-income vice (Figure 6a and b).

Figure 6: Absence of Club Convergence in Mexico—Increasing Inequalities and Drivers of Inequality and Migration—Disparities in Service Delivery

(a)

Distribution of state clubs

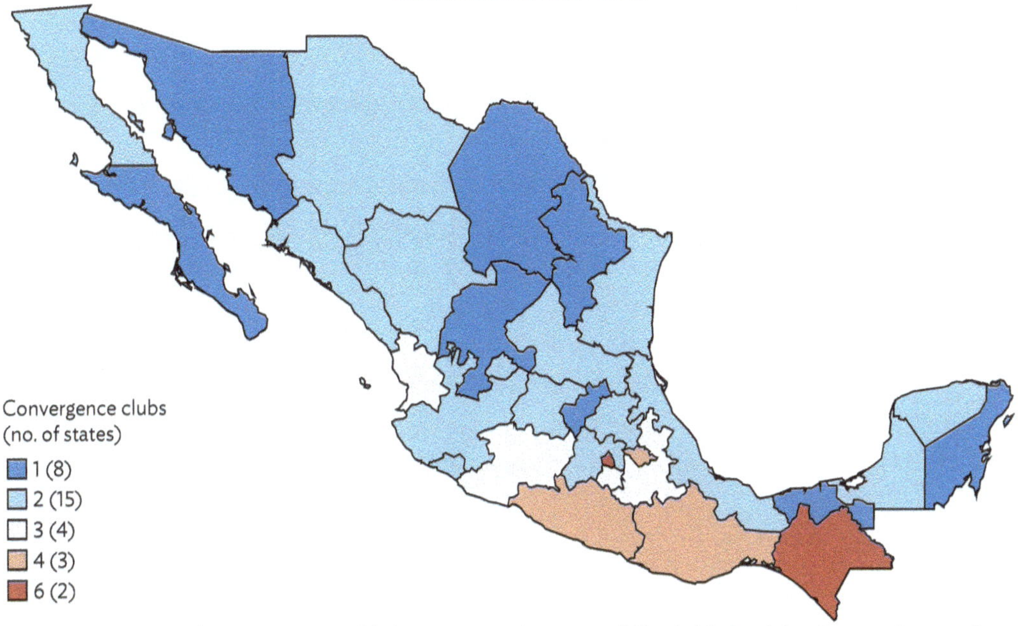

Note: Mexican states do not converge–with the proper southern states falling behind and showing negative growth.

(b)

Access to electricity + Pipe water + Drainage

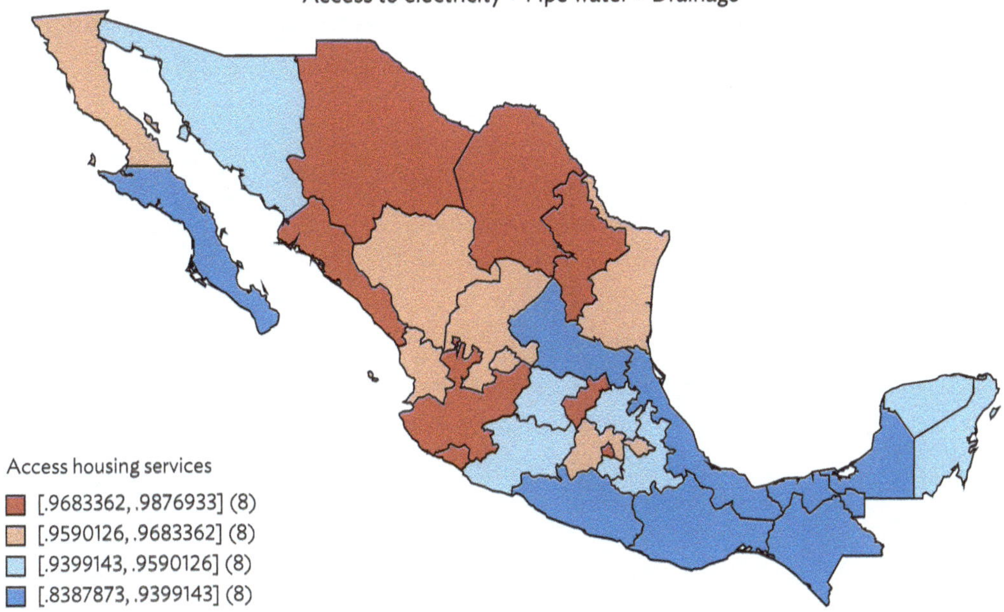

Source: Population Census 2020.

Source: E. Ahmad and H. Viscarra. 2021. *Convergence, Labor Markets and Spatial Dynamics of Urban Transformation in Mexico 2003–15.* LSE Program on Financing Sustainable Transition in China and Mexico.

People's Republic of China: Digital Transformation and Completion of Value-Added Tax Reforms (2015–2020)

The **Western Development Strategy in the PRC around 2000**, encouraged by some multilateral development banks (MDBs), focused on infrastructure gaps between the coastal and interior provinces, particularly in the lagging western provinces. This did not reverse growing inequalities across provinces or stop the flow of migrants and firms to the coastal megacities, like Guangzhou (Figure 7; Ahmad, 2021; Luo and Zhu, 2020).

The PRC's drive to bring the full BTB value chain into the VAT was driven by an increasing need to generate greater efficiency and reduce costs of doing business, and to minimize distortions in the location decisions by firms and workers. The need for covering the BTB value chain was due to rising costs and an appreciating exchange rate that could affect the competitiveness of exports. The **integration of the local business tax mainly on services with the VAT** was undertaken in 2016, and built on the solid computerized basis of the GTS that, as mentioned above, focused on matching VAT invoices, especially for the special *fapiao* (invoices).

Phase III of the GTS prepared the grounds for the exchange of information that unified and integrated national and local tax data. Electronic "e-fapiao" for business-to-consumer transactions were introduced very soon after the integration of the business tax with the VAT. However, B2B transactions could not be digitized with multiple administrations, and had to await further tax administration reforms. Small taxpayers (with annual taxable sales below CNY5 million or roughly $800,000) continued to be subject to a reduced VAT on gross sales at 3% without permitting input tax deductions.

All local tax bureau were consolidated in 2018 into a single national tax authority, the State Tax Administration (STA). Special e-fapiao were phased in from 2020 onward, with the intention of completing the full value chain nationwide by 2023/24.

An additional advantage of the e-fapiao lies **in facilitating enterprises to further automate and optimize operations**. This should help to streamline business processes for higher productivity and enhanced internal control in risk management. This will also assist with supply chain management and client relations, and facilitate procurement processes. It is, however, likely that the initial focus not to include smaller taxpayers would benefit the larger firms concentrated along the coastal seaboard and the metropolitan areas, *reinforcing existing spatial imbalances.*

Figure 7: Interprovincial- and Intra-Provincial Migratory Flows in the People's Republic of China, 2014

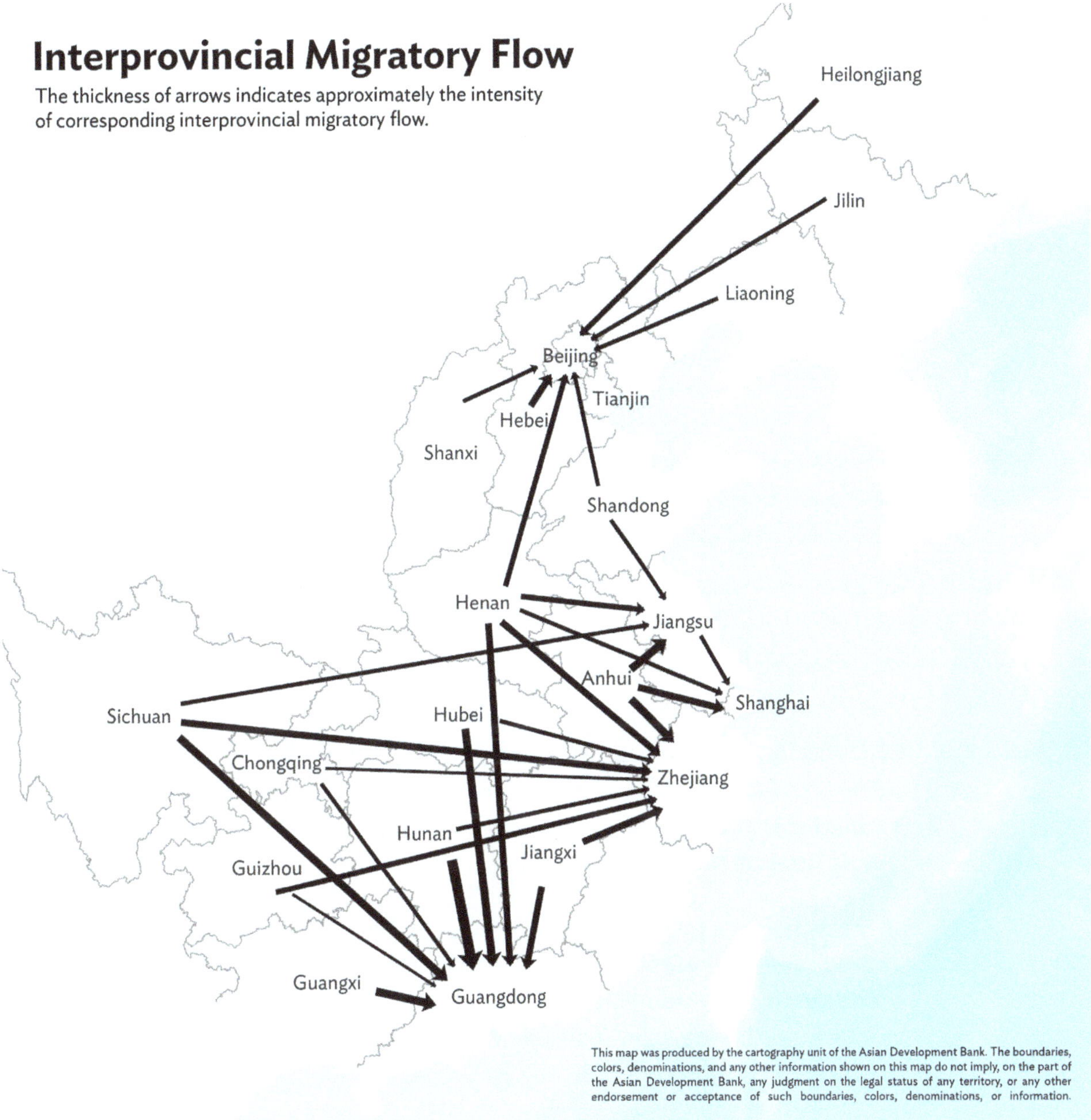

Source: X. Luo and N. Zhu. 2020. *Migration, Agglomeration and Regional Structural Transformation in China.* LSE Program on Financing Sustainable Transitions in China and Mexico; see also E. Ahmad. 2021. Multilevel financing of Sustainable Development in China: Options for Inclusive, Resilient and Green Growth. *Journal of Infrastructure and Policy Development.* 5 (1).

The digital transformation could lead to better integration of large and small firms, and is a necessary although not sufficient condition to address regional inequalities as well as imbalances between the advanced coastal areas and the lagging interior regions. "Rebalancing" has become an increasingly important focus of policymaking, e.g., in the 14th Five Year and Perspective Plans, which also introduced the concept of "dual circulation" to refer to producing and consuming domestically, while maintaining export markets with this objective and also generating greater resilience in the face of turbulence in global supply chains.

The **launch of Phase IV of the GTS** was announced to BRICS (Brazil, Russia, India, the People's Republic of China, South Africa, Iran, Egypt, Ethiopia, and the United Arab Emirates) tax authorities in September 2021, **with the intention to transition from "managing tax through invoices" to "managing tax through big data."** The STA has also become **solely responsible for collecting social insurance contributions**. The emphasis on big data will be supplemented by cloud and AI technologies. This will permit a cross sharing of information across the tax, social security, market regulators, banks, and other institutions. Full implementation of Phase IV was, however, delayed because of the COVID-19 pandemic.

Enhancing Subnational Resilience: Critical Role for State, Provincial, or Local Own-Source Tax Handles

With the centralization of wide-area taxes (VAT, excises, and income taxes) and administration reforms in both the PRC and Mexico to improve the business climate, **subnational governments are left with almost no tax bases over which they can adjust rates at the margin**.

In both countries, **financing subnational operations shifted significantly to shared revenues and intergovernmental transfers**. This does not provide adequate incentives for subnational accountability, and cannot form the basis for accessing private finance needed for sustainable investments, especially in lagging areas.

Mexican Subnational Problems

Mexico had a distorting and inefficient system of taxes at the state level (on the payroll, *nomina*), as discussed above. However, it also had **a long-standing system of US-style property tax based on ownership, market-based valuation, and land-value capture with forms of betterment levies**. This included an additional development charge, and in some states a proper betterment levy (*impuesto de plusvalia*) that are key elements of land-value capture, other than land acquisition and sales. Sales are subject to both capital gains tax and VAT.

The problem is that **the Mexican property tax, outside the main metropolitan areas like Mexico City (CDMX), has been ineffective in raising revenues—accounting for around 0.2% of GDP for almost half a century**—with almost half coming from CDMX, which has managed to update cadaster and valuations regularly. Even CDMX managed to collect only 0.44% of its GDP, largely due to the political economy problem of imposing market-based tax rates on fixed-income and liquidity-constrained households. **The land-value capture instrument, *plusvalia*, where imposed, raised virtually no revenues**.

Even if 1.5% of GDP is generated from property taxes in Mexico (roughly half of the expected potential),[21] it **would go a long way toward the pandemic recovery** and anchoring significant improvements in local services needed to attract investments, especially in the lagging regions. **Simulations for Mexican states based on a simple area-location-based model for the recurrent property tax, linked to public services,[22] show that it could be expected to raise the revenues quickly**. As the example below illustrates, this is progressive, with enhancements in local government capacity to provide the SDGs and to attract financing for infrastructure investments, and to generate greater local accountability.

In the Mexican example below, **the rate per square meter (rate/m^2) is set in relation to the built-up areas, and a broad indicator of level of development, proxied in this example by state-level GDP**. In practice, an average rate/m^2 meter for a state will probably be too low for some cities (and localities within cities) and too high for others, but is being used for purely illustrative purposes. This method sidesteps problems with complicated and expensive cadasters (that might be needed for legal purposes and for business properties), ownership, and valuation complications, and can be implemented relatively quickly.

Table 2 illustrates the method. **The simple beneficial property tax can be highly differentiated** by city (and locality, although this is not shown here) and is likely to play a **very strong role in the spatial dynamics of urban transformation** in Mexico. The tax rate/m^2 is set at 1.5% of state GDP and varies from Mex\$437/m^2 in CDMX to Mex\$88/m^2 in Chiapas.

21 R. Bahl and S. Wallace. 2008. *Reforming the Property Tax in Developing Countries. A New Approach*. Working Paper 08-19, Andrew Young School of Public Policy.

22 E. Ahmad and H. Viscarra. 2020. *Financing Clean, Compact and Connected Cities in Mexico: Role of a "Beneficial" Property Tax*. LSE/BEIS Program on Sustainable Transitions in China and Mexico. See also chapter on Mexico in E. Ahmad and G. Brosio. 2023. *Beneficial Property Taxes for Emerging Market Countries—Addressing Climate Change and Post-pandemic Recovery*. Palgrave Macmillan.

Table 2: Determining the Rate of a Beneficial Property Tax in Mexico

States	Average Property Size (m^2)	Expected Income 1.5% of GDP (millions of pesos)	Tax Mex$/Square Meter
Aguas Calientes	95.3	2.973	180.73
Baja California	83.5	7.589	201.45
Baja California Sur	72.8	1.951	245.71
Campeche	75.3	1.904	190.38
Coahuila	98.2	8.608	210.17
Colima	88.6	1.430	186.38
Chiapas	64.5	4.357	87.88
Chihuahua	102.2	7.728	190.04
CDMX	92.2	42.548	437.87
Durango	96.6	2.925	122.18
Guanajuato	96.2	9.918	134.79
Guerrero	61.9	3.480	109.61
Hidalgo	80.3	3.804	108.19
Jalisco	99.6	16.615	178.73
Mexico	77.8	21.578	115.45
Michoacan	77.7	5.875	122.13
Morelos	79.3	2.797	141.74
Nayarit	89.1	1.723	110.34
Nuevo Leon	93.1	18.289	264.25
Oaxaca	64.8	3.908	98.60
Puebla	77.9	8.092	123.49
Queretaro	88.8	5.548	211.16
Quintana Roo	69.6	3.683	255.96
Potosí	94.6	4.952	126.40
Sinaloa	72.0	5.429	161.94
Sonora	85.4	8.062	215.33
Tabasco	76.9	3.935	138.19
Tamaulipas	82.3	7.359	227.69
Tlaxcala	79.3	1.449	97.65
Veracruz	72.4	12.060	139.58
Yucatan	73.5	3.483	152.41
Zacatecas	93.1	2.388	133.93

CDMX = Mexico City, GDP = gross domestic product, m^2 = square meter.

Source: E. Ahmad and H. Viscarra. 2020. *Financing Clean, Compact and Connected Cities in Mexico: Role of a "Beneficial" Property Tax.* LSE/BEIS Program on Sustainable Transitions in China and Mexico.

The distributional consequences of the beneficial property tax in Mexico are striking. The inequality effect is calculated for low, medium, and higher levels of inequality aversion (e = 0.5, 1, and 2, respectively), and compares the origin level of inequality without tax (Y_0), the tax on its own (Y_1), and with the tax distributed equally (Y_2), or to families with children for education and/or health spending. The tax on its own reduces inequality in most states—most markedly for Chiapas—and the effect is magnified as the benefit linkages are introduced, and inequality aversion increased (Table 3). Given the importance of the poor people in Chiapas, this is a very powerful result.

The CDMX case is of interest. The tax on its own increases inequality at low levels of inequality aversion. However, the situation changes when linked to benefits targeted to children—in this case for education. However, for moderate or high levels of inequality aversion, the tax on its own reduces inequality in CDMX, and the impact of linkage with either equal distribution of benefits, or targeted to education is even stronger.

Clearly, **the tax-benefit linkage is a very powerful policy tool for a government that is very concerned with inequality and creating sustainable employment hubs**. The effective provision of basic services is critical to attract both firms and workers, especially in the lagging southern states of the country.[23] This is of particular relevance to countries such as the PRC and Indonesia trying to shift activities from congested metropolitan areas to lagging regions.

Relative to the current collection of 0.26% of GDP on account of the property tax, **the proposed 1.5% of state revenues on average would give a tremendous boost to the own-source revenue potential in every state**. This would open the doors to a more systematic use of private finance for public infrastructure, including green bonds, without exacerbating risks from subnational liabilities.

The most significant increases in revenue potential are in CDMX as well as Chiapas. This makes the reform of interest in both rich and poorer states. However, the tax potential in CDMX is almost 10 times the revenues that could accrue to Chiapas (Table 6) and twice the revenue potential of the measure in the State of Mexico (the next highest).

In order to prevent the measure from increasing spatial inequality and reversing the dynamics of urban transformation, it is important to pose the reforms jointly with a modern fiscal equalization reworking of the *Participaciones*, as recommended in Ahmad et al. (2007). ***This is essential for rebalancing and employment generation in the poorer regions of the country***.

23 E. Ahmad, J.L. Añorve, and H. Viscarra. 2021. *Productivity Enhancement and Sustainable Employment in Mexico: Building Forward Better from the Pandemic and Creating Inclusive Growth*. ILO ACT/EMP.

Table 3: Mexican States: Initial Distribution of Income and Distributional Impact of Area-Based Property Tax, and Links to Basic Services for Different Levels of Inequality Aversion

	e = 0.5				e = 1				e = 2			
States	Y_0	Y_1 (Y_0 - property tax 1.5% GDP)	Y_2 (target)	Y_2 (equal)	Y_0	Y_1 (Y_0 - property tax 1.5% GDP)	Y_2 (target)	Y_2 (equal)	Y_0	Y_1 (Y_0 - property tax 1.5% GDP)	Y_2 (target)	Y_2 (equal)
Aguas Calientes	0.152	0.160	0.09	0.134	0.297	0.308	0.176	0.261	0.541	0.55	0.338	0.477
Baja California	0.204	0.215	0.154	0.188	0.353	0.373	0.255	0.325	0.574	0.598	0.375	0.515
Baja California Sur	0.185	0.219	0.132	0.208	0.331	0.382	0.244	0.367	0.539	0.59	0.42	0.576
Campeche	0.271	0.219	0.085	0.166	0.431	0.379	0.158	0.289	0.618	0.585	0.281	0.458
Coahuila	0.186	0.135	0.066	0.121	0.334	0.264	0.125	0.242	0.555	0.484	0.225	0.464
Colima	0.167	0.172	0.081	0.148	0.304	0.313	0.154	0.269	0.519	0.52	0.282	0.448
Chiapas	0.436	0.246	0.08	0.14	0.620	0.450	0.155	0.261	0.807	0.72	0.287	0.456
Chihuahua	0.195	0.158	0.078	0.133	0.351	0.301	0.142	0.250	0.569	0.531	0.241	0.437
CDMX	0.148	0.151	0.144	0.151	0.278	0.277	0.263	0.275	0.496	0.467	0.436	0.461
Durango	0.172	0.166	0.063	0.129	0.316	0.322	0.125	0.252	0.541	0.584	0.244	0.464
Guanajuato	0.168	0.154	0.091	0.116	0.317	0.289	0.162	0.219	0.569	0.517	0.271	0.395
Guerrero	0.206	0.177	0.068	0.131	0.385	0.354	0.13	0.262	0.634	0.634	0.234	0.485
Hidalgo	0.239	0.283	0.099	0.203	0.426	0.490	0.172	0.346	0.683	0.761	0.278	0.528
Jalisco	0.170	0.172	0.141	0.144	0.314	0.315	0.248	0.265	0.553	0.554	0.395	0.469
Mexico	0.191	0.182	0.157	0.139	0.354	0.344	0.289	0.265	0.599	0.604	0.48	0.476
Michoacan	0.228	0.226	0.109	0.171	0.404	0.404	0.192	0.309	0.642	0.635	0.308	0.508
Morelos	0.222	0.254	0.132	0.206	0.387	0.456	0.234	0.369	0.615	0.717	0.379	0.594
Nayarit	0.201	0.221	0.113	0.186	0.366	0.403	0.215	0.340	0.619	0.684	0.417	0.597
Nuevo Leon	0.162	0.154	0.126	0.139	0.295	0.284	0.226	0.257	0.494	0.475	0.362	0.442
Oaxaca	0.230	0.221	0.089	0.158	0.428	0.421	0.178	0.307	0.703	0.723	0.364	0.573
Puebla	0.285	0.225	0.121	0.171	0.461	0.403	0.211	0.312	0.688	0.656	0.336	0.527
Queretaro	0.199	0.203	0.104	0.166	0.363	0.374	0.193	0.307	0.627	0.657	0.35	0.546
Quintana Roo	0.149	0.149	0.07	0.132	0.286	0.278	0.138	0.250	0.525	0.472	0.269	0.441
Potosí	0.274	0.247	0.13	0.205	0.486	0.449	0.23	0.370	0.748	0.72	0.378	0.602
Sinaloa	0.175	0.188	0.075	0.155	0.335	0.351	0.14	0.292	0.585	0.583	0.246	0.494
Sonora	0.190	0.188	0.12	0.168	0.331	0.327	0.202	0.293	0.536	0.536	0.311	0.48
Tabasco	0.213	0.206	0.106	0.172	0.392	0.391	0.206	0.333	0.654	0.677	0.407	0.607
Tamaulipas	0.190	0.191	0.122	0.168	0.346	0.354	0.222	0.311	0.584	0.59	0.363	0.517
Tlaxcala	0.184	0.182	0.084	0.134	0.340	0.349	0.166	0.256	0.597	0.643	0.323	0.466
Veracruz	0.248	0.217	0.152	0.174	0.423	0.390	0.259	0.315	0.659	0.648	0.399	0.528
Yucatan	0.237	0.241	0.106	0.191	0.415	0.422	0.189	0.338	0.658	0.65	0.31	0.531
Zacatecas	0.309	0.212	0.077	0.154	0.470	0.369	0.152	0.276	0.655	0.613	0.309	0.48

CDMX = Mexico City, GDP = gross domestic product.

Source: E. Ahmad and H. Viscarra. 2020. *Financing Clean, Compact and Connected Cities in Mexico: Role of a "Beneficial" Property Tax*. LSE/BEIS Program on Sustainable Transitions in China and Mexico.

Despite the success in integrating small taxpayers into the VAT net, **Mexico's potential to build on a broader tax reform agenda is limited by the absence of a unique NID number**. In this regard, Mexico trails countries like India and the PRC.

People's Republic of China—Local Finances for "Rebalancing" and Addressing the Property Crisis

The COVID-19 pandemic has highlighted **the interconnected problems of inadequate local government financing, incentives to engage in off-budget borrowing and greater reliance on land sales, and pressures on property developers and the property crisis**. The structural imbalances are particularly acute in Tier III cities and below in the interior provinces, and **jeopardize the objectives of "rebalancing" activities** to CCCs, and the "dual circulation" in the 14th Five Year Plan to shift toward domestic consumption and production rather than exports.

The **efficiency-driven integration of the VAT and local business tax regime led to the subsequent creation of the STA serving all levels of government** (absorbing all local tax administrations). Consequently, local governments have become increasingly reliant on shared revenues, despite central government guidance doubling down on land sales and off-budget transactions, including borrowing, of the urban development investment corporations (UDICs). Significant rate cuts in broad-based taxes, as part of the central government's countercyclical policies during the pandemic, have heightened the budgetary pressure on local governments, leading to adverse incentives to increase land sales and engage in "disguised" borrowing.

With the rational **integration of the VAT base and rate structure, together with effective centralization of all wide-area taxes and administration, Chinese local governments are increasingly reliant on shared revenues and transfers**. Attempts to pilot the ownership-valuation property tax in Shanghai and Chongqing failed to raise revenues. Local governments used land sales to generate funds for expansion and infrastructure.

While the drawbacks to the land sales model have been apparent to the authorities, it has proved hard to eliminate it given the pressures on local government. The land sales **fueled significant urban sprawl**. Much of this urban expansion has been at the expense of productive agricultural land or fragile ecosystems such as deltas, increasing exposure to natural hazards (Wang, Wu, and Ye, 2018). Moreover, the off-budget nature of the revenues generated, with weak monitoring, has fueled rent-seeking behavior at the local levels.

More important is the increase in fiscal risks, given the rise of off-budget borrowing through the UDICs leveraging land sales. Local governments were prohibited from borrowing to meet current spending before 2015. However, their UDICs **could borrow using local government financing vehicles (LGFVs) for capital investments**—the so-called "golden rule." This policy was not always followed in reality, and the UDICs provided convenient off-budget funding for all sorts of spending. In response to the global financial crisis in 2008–2010, the central government used the UDICs and LGFVs used to finance the CNY4-trillion stimulus. The consequent spiraling of subnational liabilities has become a matter for urgent concern for the central government **and developing an effective system of local taxation was a priority for the 14th Five Year Plan**.

As indicated above, Chinese **local government "officially recognized" that debt increased significantly in the post-2010 period**, as part of the central government's countercyclical measures in the face of the global economic downturn. However, this also added to the opaque magnitude of existing local government liabilities. In response to international financial institution (IFI) advice, the PRC moved to replace the cumulative **bank debt by local government bonds, designed to introduce a more orderly instrument that would also begin to utilize the PRC's accumulated savings**. However, the change in the budget law to permit effective local government borrowing was followed almost immediately in 2015 by the integration of the local business tax on services with the national VAT in order to reduce the cost of doing business. With incomplete balance sheets (in a small city in central PRC, the true magnitude of liabilities in 2019 was a multiple of the amounts declared)[24] and no effective own-source revenues (note that shared revenues and transfers do not count for this purpose—see Box), consequently, there is no hard-budget constraint. **A local government bond system merely enhanced the potential of a debt spiral facing many local governments**.

There is a **presumption that infrastructure financed by project bonds linked to tolls or user charges, without guarantees, need not be counted as public debt**. This applied to the 1990s road-building program in Mexico—financed by state banks linked to toll revenues, but with no federal or state guarantees, as described also in Box. The economic shock of the "tequila crisis" had a knock-on effect on toll revenues, and to the ability of the firms to service debts to the banks, adding greatly to the banking crisis that required a federal bailout and effectively became a subnational debt crisis.

24 E. Ahmad and X. Zhang. 2020. *Local Government Liabilities and Sustainable Debt in China: The Role of Balance Sheet Information—Evidence From County-level City T in Central China*. LSE Program on Financing Sustainable Urban Transitions in China and Mexico.

Box: Why Sustainable Subnational Debt Issuance Requires Own-Source Revenues

The issue of subnational debt sustainability has been subject to a great deal of debate including in the European Union. The fiscal rules and debt break imposed a zero-borrowing limit on the Länder (states in Germany), as they have no own-source revenues.[a] The fiscal rules have been suspended because of the pandemic, and there is some discussion as to what should follow so as not to discourage investment. Some argue that a "golden rule" might be more appropriate—and this would be the equivalent of the **special bond issuance for investment purposes in the People's Republic of China (PRC)**. However, the golden rule is hard to define precisely, and it is unlikely that project-related bonds or public–private partnerships (PPPs) will avert budget recourse. This was seen in Spain in 2008 and the Mexican road-financing disaster during the "tequila crisis" of the 1990s, when local project liabilities contributed to a banking crisis that needed to be bailed out by the central government. The problem is magnified exponentially with weak subnational public finance management and incomplete information that generate soft-budget constraints. In the PRC, the post-1993/94 local government financing vehicles were meant to follow a golden rule but also became a major source of risk. The argument can be summarized as follows:

Start with the "Simonsen rule" for debt sustainability. For national governments, this links changes in liabilities ∂L to changes in revenue raising potential ∂R:

$$\partial L = f(\partial R)$$

where,

$$\partial R = \partial t.\ \partial B$$

where, t is the set of tax instruments and B is the base. The Simonsen rule then translates into the famous relationship between the interest rate and the growth rate of the economy driving the revenue base in the medium term. For subnational governments (subscript s), the subnational R_s can be decomposed:

$$t_s B_s + \rho B_n$$

where, t_s is own-source taxes in relation to a subnational tax base (B_s) and ρB_n is the share of national taxes meant to cover assigned spending E_s. In the Chinese intergovernmental settlement post-1993/94, the revenue shares were meant to cover a set of agreed expenditures given the effective centralization of revenue bases, and to close the resulting vertical gap. Consequently, there is little flexibility in reality.

Thus, in the Chinese provinces, $t_s = 0$, and $\rho b_n - E_s = 0$, even if the share of national revenues is untied, so the first difference of available revenues is zero. Consequently, without own-source revenues, the sustainable level ∂L_s of subnational debt in the PRC is zero (regardless of the type of local bond issuance).

The even greater earmarking that has emerged from the current "decentralization" effort further reduces the ability of local governments to meet debt liabilities and finance basic public services. Consequently, the incentives for local government are to continue to incur debt, especially through special instruments and PPPs that are not so easy to monitor, significantly adding to overall risk. While these pressures are seen, in the metropolitan regions (e.g., Guangzhou) and capital city clusters (e.g., Nanchang), the most severe effects are on the Tier III and Tier IV cities and could prevent them from becoming clean, compact, and connected "sustainable hubs."

[a] E. Ahmad, M. Bordignon, and G. Brosio. 2016. *Multilevel finance and the Eurocrisis*. Edward Elgar.

Source: E. Ahmad. 2021. Multilevel financing of Sustainable Development in China: Options for Inclusive, Resilient and Green Growth. *Journal of Infrastructure and Policy Development*. 5 (1).

While it is important to utilize local government bonds (including green bonds) and public–private partnerships (PPPs) in financing and managing key infrastructure projects at the local and city levels, **key preconditions must be met to avoid increasing the risk of unsustainable debt**:

- at the margin, **some control over local tax rates** is needed (see Box and Ambrosanio and Bordignon, 2015); as well as
- **full disclosure of liabilities in balance sheets** compatible with the IMF's Government Finance Statistics Manual standard.

With PPPs, the correct procedure is that assets that revert to the state must be accounted for on the balance sheet of the respective governments with adequate provisioning.

It is clearly appropriate to set up a **local government bond system as part of the development of sustainable financial instruments available** in any country, especially given the magnitude of investments needed for sustainable growth and addressing climate risks, but the preconditions and sequencing matter greatly. Inadequately prepared measures copied from the US can lead to "good intentions, bad outcomes." Again, there are lessons from both the PRC and Mexico for each other and emerging-market countries, in general.

Despite attempts to discourage land sales and imposing prudential limits on property developers (the three red lines), the pressure on local budgets has increased with the pandemic. This has been exacerbated by the countercyclical policies of the central government, that in turn telescope pressures on shared revenues for local governments. Thus, the incentive to rely at the margin on land sales, including indirect borrowings by UDICs, has if anything increased. The pressures have resulted in financial distress of many large developers, including Country Wide—one of the biggest property developers—and the bankruptcy of Evergrande.

The budgetary and structural problems are magnified in Tier III and smaller towns, where population continues to decline—even in provinces like Henan and Sichuan where the capital cities, Zhengzhou and Chengdu, continue to grow.[25] This trend is indicated in local governments' resident data for 2023, and the migrations continue toward the Greater Bay Area (GBA) and the Yangtze River Delta.[26] The migration of the younger and better-qualified workers is because of better job prospects, wages, and public services in these areas. The smaller cities are further disadvantaged by shrinking and aging local populations, and inability to finance commensurate public services.

25 Henan province population fell by 570,000 in 2023, while the capital Zhengzhou (where Apple's iPhones are assembled) grew by 180,000 new residents. Sichuan province overall population declined by 60,000, while its capital Chengdu attracted 135,000 new residents.

26 The population in Zhejiang province grew by 500,000 in 2023, and Guangdong province by 490,000 in 2023.

This **further reduces the attractiveness of Tier III cities, especially in the interior, for firms that might otherwise have relocated away from the congested coastal metropolises, exacerbating the spatial inequalities** that have arisen, as seen in the 2010 floating population trends (Figure 7).

Beneficial Property Tax Option for the People's Republic of China

As in the Mexico case, Ahmad et al. (2019) examine the effects of a recurrent beneficial property tax for the PRC using a simple design based on area, location, and occupancy (footnote 25). As argued by Alfred Marshall during the 19th century, political opposition is reduced with the **direct linkage to benefits,** for example, for education or social housing. The local **setting of rates within a centrally determined band** (already in place for taxation of property sales in the PRC) is important in creating stable own-source revenue for local governments, and this is critical for reducing risks associated with the buildup of local liabilities (Ahmad, 2018). Also, an objective of the reform is to make it more attractive for lower-income and less-skilled workers to move to cheaper, interior cities, and to attract more labor-intensive activities away from the GBA (e.g., textiles, rather than moving to Bangladesh or Viet Nam). The beneficial property tax can play a signaling role in this context—generating less congestion and pollution in the GBA, and CCCs in the interior in Tier III cities.

In the PRC, **the area-based approach is a suitable option because of the complexity of the housing stock**—a large share of privatized public housing stock, from previous state-owned enterprises and public sector units, was made available on a restricted leasehold basis—**and possible distortion of property valuations given the extensive involvement of local governments in property development**. The property value information collected in the 2016 survey is based on households' own assessments, which can be highly unreliable because of the complexity discussed above. For example, many properties bought from the previous state-owned enterprises at heavily discounted prices often were in premium locations, but they could not be freely traded in the property market due to complexity of ownership titles. While the purchase price is an underestimate of property value, there is no effective free market price either. This adds to the political economy difficulty with the ownership–valuation model experiments in Shanghai and Chongqing.

The **following analysis adopts the area-based assessment method for a property tax and distributional impacts of alternative formulations of the proposal are illustrated through policy simulations** using China Labor Urban Survey data for six major cities. Although positive effects on income distribution would be more marked by targeting migrant and low-income households, overall political acceptability is increased if all the population were to benefit from the tax (Ahmad et al., 2020) (footnote 25). Also, it is likely that in the PRC, the beneficial property tax revenues will flow to municipal budgets and then to basic spending requirements such as education or health care that are provided free, and hence do not appear in household surveys. While the policy simulations use measurable variables, the main objective of a "beneficial" property tax is precisely to ensure that the city or county government pays attention to say "preventive health care" (as in Wuhan in the run up to the pandemic), for which there is also broad public support.

The distributional impact analysis is carried out using a policy simulation exercise; and to focus on the "gainers and losers" story we assume that all beneficial property tax revenue is distributed for specific benefit. We assess distributional consequences sequentially to illustrate the individual as well as the combined effect of a property tax and social spending on income inequality. This involves the construction of three income variables. The "initial income" (Y_0) is the recorded household income, net of income tax and social security contribution; the "disposable income" (Y_d) is estimated after deducting a property tax; and the "final income" (Y_f) is constructed by adding social transfers (education and housing subsidies) to Y_d.

Key steps and assumptions imposed in the simulations follow. **The first step focuses on setting a tax rate**. In theory, a city-specific property tax rate should be set, based on the principles of equity, administrative simplicity, and fiscal sustainability. In the latter case, local governments should set the rate to reflect its assessment of spending needs (proposed services) and associated costs. For simplicity, we estimate the **tax rate under the assumption that all cities set the rate to raise local revenue to a level of 2% of local GDP, to provide somewhat more revenues than land sales that would be phased out**. This is also a benchmark based on the median property tax revenue as a share of GDP across OECD countries, and a lower bound to the World Bank estimates for emerging-market property tax potential mentioned above (Bahl and Wallace, 2008).

In the second step, **child and education transfers are estimated for each city based on current city-level per capita education spending**.[27] All migrant households with children of school age are provided with transfers. In a second iteration, we allocate funds for all children as a form of child benefit (this is appropriate since all cities run deficits, and education spending in particular presents financing difficulties for cities with mandates and no own-source revenues, e.g., Nanchang). Finally, all low-income households, defined as those with per capita incomes below 50% of the city-level median income, are provided with transfers for education or housing.

27 The method for estimating the benefit from public education spending consists of imputing a value to the benefit accrued to an individual of going to public schools that equals the per-beneficiary input costs obtained from administrative data for individual cities.

It is interesting that the **2% of GDP level more or less covers the education spending** in each of the capital cities, other than Shanghai (Table 4). Shanghai, of course, is a metropolitan city with provincial status and thus also benefits from a full share of the VAT (higher than the other capital cities). The considerably greater spending on education also probably explains the very strong performance of Shanghai in the global OECD Programme for International Student Assessment (PISA) rankings.

Table 4: Simulations of Property Tax of 2% of GDP and Education Spending, People's Republic of China

City	Property Tax 2% GDP (CNY billion)	Current Education Spending (CNY billion)	Property Tax (CNY/m^2)
Guangzhou	39.2	32.12	121.4
Shanghai	54.9	84.10	90.81
Shenyang	10.9	11.51	52.68
Wuhan	23.8	23.11	85.11
Xian	12.5	11.96	48.8
Fuzhou	12.4	15.31	54.6

m^2 = square meter, GDP = gross domestic product.
Source: E. Ahmad and G. Brosio, 2022. *Financing Sustainable Local Spending and Infrastructure in China*. Springer Books. in: Beneficial Property Taxation for Emerging Market Countries. pp. 61-91. Springer.

The assessment of the distributional consequences is based on two most commonly used inequality measures—the Gini coefficient and Atkinson index.[28] While the Gini coefficient is more widely used, it is most sensitive to income changes in the middle segment of the income distribution. This typically reflects preferences of policy makers in a large number of countries. The Atkinson index permits the weights on different segments of the distribution of income to vary from 0 (zero), where equal weights are given to all segments of the population and no preference to any group, to higher values say on the impact on poorer groups. Inequality aversion parameters of 0.5–1 reflect the preferences of most distributionally inclined governments, and more or less mirrors the Gini coefficient. In order to focus on the lowest end of the size distribution, we also use an inequality aversion parameter of 2 for the Atkinson index. This focuses attention on poorer households, such as migrants in most cities. However, one has to be careful, as not all migrants are poor. In Guangzhou, migrants from other cities have more or less the same per capita incomes as residents and are equally likely to have above average living space, considerably higher than the poorest groups, which might include migrants from rural areas (for details, see Ahmad et al., 2020) (footnote 25).

28 The Atkinson index allows different weights on relative positions in the income distribution, given by a coefficient, labeled as e, that reflects the level of "inequality aversion." The greater the weight on the inequality aversion parameter, the more sensitive Atkinson index (e) is to income differences at the bottom of the distribution. Common choices of e range from 0 to 2, where 0 implies that a yuan to the poorest is treated the same as a yuan to the richest (zero inequality aversion), and 2 puts almost exclusive weight on the poorest.

Table 5 presents **the initial distributional impact for three scenarios of policy changes for six cities which result in different distributional impacts (income levels Y_j)**:

(i) Gini coefficient and Atkinson index at initial level (Y_0);

(ii) Gini coefficient and Atkinson index with imposition of an area-based property tax (Y_1);

(iii) Gini coefficient and Atkinson index with property tax combined with education subsidies (Y_2); and

(iv) Gini coefficient and Atkinson index with property tax combined with education and social housing subsidies (Y_3).

The variance in tax rates by a city provides a system of market-based incentives to limit migration to the mega-metropolises along the coast. On its own, the tax has no impact on the Gini coefficient relative to the status quo in each case, although the introduction of a housing benefit in addition to the social benefit reduces inequality in Shanghai. The Gini coefficient is more reflective of changes in the middle ranges of the income distribution and reflects **the "middle class" outcomes that typically drive the political economy responses. The reform itself does not pose significant problems from this perspective, and any negative impact is completely offset with the "beneficial" linkages.**

A **different inequality measurement index can focus on the effects of the tax alone on the poorest groups**. The Atkinson index, with a relatively high inequality aversion parameter (e = 2), places greater weight on the bottom end of the size distribution. Here there are different impacts, probably reflecting the weight of the migrant populations in each of the metropolitan areas. In Guangzhou and Shenyang, **the tax alone reduces the Atkinson index** significantly (see Y_1 relative to Y_0 in Table 5). The Wuhan case is of particular interest—where there was a huge increase in migrants into Wuhan during 2010–2015, both at the lower end of the income spectrum and also among higher income groups. The influence of the latter is seen in the imposition of the tax relative to the status quo—it reduces inequality. Because the targeting of migrants also includes rich households, the provision of a benefit to migrants in this case *actually increases* inequality. This is not the case in most other cities but it does point to the need for care in establishing the benefit criteria linked to the benefit tax.

Table 5: Distributional Impact of the Beneficial Property Tax Options

	Atkinson Index				Gini Coefficient			
	Y_0	Y_1	Y_2	Y_3	Y_0	Y_1	Y_2	Y_3
Guangzhou	0.60	0.76	0.75	0.74	0.39	0.40	0.40	0.39
Shanghai	0.72	0.51	0.49	0.44	0.40	0.41	0.40	0.40
Shenyang	0.63	0.49	0.49	0.45	0.33	0.34	0.34	0.33
Wuhan	0.52	0.48	0.48	0.60	0.33	0.35	0.34	0.34
Xian	0.47	0.58	0.51	0.41	0.35	0.36	0.35	0.35
Fuzhou	0.51	0.89	0.90	0.89	0.36	0.37	0.37	0.37

Note: The simulation assumes providing education (Y1) and housing (Y2) subsidy only to migrant households.

	Atkinson Index				Gini Coefficient			
	Y_0	Y_1	Y_2	Y_3	Y_0	Y_1	Y_2	Y_3
Guangzhou	0.60	0.76	0.76	0.74	0.39	0.40	0.40	0.40
Shanghai	0.72	0.51	0.50	0.46	0.40	0.41	0.41	0.40
Shenyang	0.63	0.49	0.48	0.44	0.33	0.34	0.33	0.33
Wuhan	0.52	0.48	0.47	0.59	0.33	0.35	0.34	0.34
Xian	0.47	0.58	0.49	0.39	0.35	0.36	0.35	0.35
Fuzhou	0.51	0.89	0.55	0.54	0.36	0.37	0.37	0.37

Note: The simulation assumes providing education (Y1) and housing (Y2) subsidy to all low-income households.
Source: Ahmad, Brosio, and Poschl (2015).

There are no major negative distributional impacts of the beneficial property tax, and the provision of a housing subsidy to poor households is strongly redistributive. Shenzhen is focusing on social housing and an interface with the income tax and benefit system is desirable. **Giving local exemptions could give rise to the "game play and corruption"** that bedevils the property tax in many emerging-market countries and should be avoided (Ahmad, Brosio, and Pöschl, 2015).

Implementing a Beneficial Property Tax in Guangzhou

A major problem in Guangzhou is that the budget has fixed and increasing spending requirements on basic services and debt financing, but the bulk of revenues are shares of national collections. The recent rational countercyclical policies of the central government to offset economic downturns and trade shocks has a negative impact on the metropolitan area's budget envelope, forcing the Guangzhou administration to revert to land sales, despite the guidance to phase out this form of financing. Although the focus in this paper is on the beneficial property tax, Ahmad (2018) has argued also to extend the piggyback principle on the personal income tax (PIT), with STA administration. This would also establish a desirable link between the city-level taxation of fixed assets and the information needed to grow the PIT base.

A second benefit is that if any rebates or benefits are applied in the Guangzhou context to the beneficial property tax, these can be offset against the sums due against the PIT piggyback (the rebates could also be applied to the current PIT share).

We briefly examine, in this section, the budgets of Guangzhou districts, focusing mainly on education expenditures. We assume that revenues from the beneficial property tax will accrue fully to the metropolitan area, and any distributional issues with fixed- or low-income households will be addressed through the income tax–benefit system, as in the UK—either to the current PIT share or an eventual Guangzhou piggyback on the PIT. An examination of the budgets of Guangzhou's 11 districts is instructive (Table 6).

A 2%-of-GDP property tax would generate more than enough revenues (CNY39 billion) to cover education spending in all districts (CNY24.01 billion), but with insufficient funding in the poorest three districts, and just about enough in five others. The bulk of the surplus would be generated in three of the richest districts and would also permit expansion of the remit to, say, housing. However, this would require a within-Guangzhou equalization mechanism to permit all districts to finance a similar level of service delivery at the same level of tax effort.

Thus, with a metropolitan-level equalization function it should be possible to fund all education and increase that in the poorer districts, and also anchor other activities such as access to private finance for public investments consistent with a sustainable growth strategy.

Table 6: Applying the Property Tax in Guangzhou Districts to Financing Education, 2016
(CNY billion)

Districts	2% GDP Property Tax	Education Spending	Surplus/Deficit in Financing
Tianhe	7.60	2.43	5.18
Huangpu	6.01	2.17	3.84
Yuexiu	5.82	2.03	3.79
Panyu	3.51	2.69	0.81
Baiyun	3.28	2.66	0.63
Haizhu	3.10	2.08	1.02
Nansha	2.56	1.00	1.56
Huadu	2.34	2.24	0.10
Liwan	2.16	2.35	(0.19)
Zengcheng	2.09	2.63	(0.53)
Congua	0.75	1.73	(0.98)

GDP = gross domestic product.
Source: Final Account Reports 2016, all 11 districts.

Lessons for Asian Countries from the People's Republic of China–Mexico Juxtaposition

The PRC–Mexico comparisons illustrate the **need for domestic resource mobilization (DRM) reforms across different political systems and unitary or federal states, and that similar instruments and policies have been utilized,** with some exchange of learning across continents. In both the PRC and Mexico, **major structural change was initiated by the policy and digital transformation opportunities associated with a VAT**. This also led to concomitant changes in tax administration design.

The **Chinese digital transformation and tax agenda differs in important aspects from that in Mexico**. With the Golden Tax System (GTS), there was relatively little leakage from the VAT in the PRC, with a C-efficiency of approximately 0.8 (OECD, 2022) relative to Mexico's 0.22 prior to the 2013 reforms. However, the multiple tax administrations and size of the country required a slower digital roll out than in Mexico, and the integration of tax administrations in 2018 was a step toward addressing this constraint. This also affects the speed and sequencing of integrating small taxpayers into the full VAT regime. The delay in full integration has a number of consequences:

- **Leaves open a door for "escaping the tax net"** as was the case in Mexico.
- **Creates disincentives for small firms to use digital tools, leading to breaks in the digital value chain**—a problem in many Asian countries from Pakistan to the Philippines.
- **The potential efficiency gains for small taxpayers including in the lagging and interior regions** would be lost, including weaker prospects for integration with global value chains that were very important in Mexico during the COVID-19 pandemic and subsequently.
- **This might increase incentives for firms and workers to remain in large metropolitan areas and coastal provinces**. Many of the large firms benefiting from the more productive value chains tend to be located there, and higher-skilled workers tend to migrate to these areas, where the jobs are located. As a corollary, many of the smaller firms that might be expected to provide significant employment opportunities in interior cities are disadvantaged. Both would limit the scope for the desired "rebalancing" toward domestic consumption and reducing spatial imbalance.

Further progress with the **digital transformation of the Mexican tax system, especially for income taxes, will depend greatly on whether a unique individual NID** can be established. This could then potentially link with digital transformation of the real and financial sectors and payment systems, along the lines suggested by Carstens and Nilekani (2024).

However, there are **many similarities between Mexican and Chinese policy reforms and digital transformations**.

- **The VAT integration of goods and services in the PRC in 2016 was expected to lose revenue,** given the additional refunds and credits due to service inputs, particularly for export-oriented sectors that were the objective of the reform. **However, overall revenue collections actually rose as a result of the reforms, as tax-on-tax interactions led to an increase in corporate income tax (CIT) revenues,** as in Mexico.

- In the PRC, as in Mexico, the **completion of the VAT value chain on goods and the taxation of services permitted the removal of boundaries around the SEZs**. This is a key element in establishing the system of cross-jurisdictional networks—including the GBA and Yangtze River Delta high-tech zones.

- **A similar cross-state high-tech transformation is possible in Mexico, linking the research and development capabilities in CDMX, the State of Mexico, and Querétaro**. As in the PRC case, environmental and distributional objectives would be met through a relocation of labor-intensive activities to southern states, including Tabasco and Chiapas, with **employment linkages with the proposed "Northern Triangle" of Central American states**.

- A full and non-distorting VAT is likely essential to **make the best use of the base erosion and profit shifting (BEPS) agenda in the future**, as FDI will depend to a large extent on the efficiency of supply chains and not tax exemptions.

- In both countries, **work is needed to develop a set of subnational own-source revenues for greater accountability and sustainable access to private financing**:

    - For state or provincial infrastructure, a piggyback on the income tax is preferable to an origin-based revenue share (the PRC already operates a version of nested piggybacks on property sales).

    - For city or local governments, the beneficial property tax holds great promise, in that it can be implemented quickly, with major distributional benefits. This is also key to solving the PRC property crisis and deleveraging the liabilities generated by the property developers.

- In keeping **with the enhancements in digital payments and settlement systems (e.g., Pix in Brazil) that considerably simplify contracts, the property-based tax system could utilize blockchain alternatives** (Ahmad and Brosio, 2022) to streamline the tax administration and information flows.

Section IV

Digitization and Value-Added Tax Integration in Other Asian Countries

Federal Countries in South Asia

The tax systems in both India and Pakistan are derived from the **colonial Government of India Act 1935 (GOI 1935), that assigned split revenue handles to elected provincial (state) governments, while keeping the main revenue heads in the center**. Thus, taxation of (final point) sales and income from agriculture and property was assigned to the provinces, while taxation of income from firms was kept in the hands of the center (colonial crown). Together with controlling taxation of international trade and excises, this was to protect British industry and commercial interests (Kumar, 1982). The agricultural income tax, which had been one of the main revenue heads to that time, collapsed since the largely rural elites that dominated the provincial legislatures had no interest in taxing themselves. This result was potentially an objective of the GOI 1935 as it increased their dependency on the crown, and was intended to perpetuate colonial rule.

At independence, **the sales tax on goods was centralized in Pakistan—as the federal government at the time had relatively few sources of revenue**. This led to further stresses on the federation, as the corresponding transfer mechanisms penalized provinces, particularly the Eastern Province (Ahmad, 2024), aimed at keeping revenues at the center. The potential advantage of laying the basis for a centrally managed VAT was lost, as the sales tax on services was assigned to the provinces under the 1973 Constitution. This reversed the arrangement envisaged in the GOI 1935, as the taxation of goods was assigned to the provinces. With the government sales tax (GST), implemented under duress under an IMF program in 1990, this split has become untenable, and is a major constraint to investment and revenue-enhancing tax reforms.

India embarked on the VAT road after Pakistan, with the split base (goods remaining with the states, as under GOI 1935) and services with the Union (central) Government. While this was easier to manage than administering services in states (provinces in Pakistan), disputes arose concerning whether items were to be classified as goods or services (Ahmad and Poddar, 2011), and the multiple administrations and myriad rate structures generated a cost to doing business.

It is interesting that the Mexican and Chinese integration of the VAT base was followed by a similar effort in India. India carried out a constitutional amendment in 2016 to integrate the VAT on goods and services assigned to different levels of government. This was a stand-alone reform that did not involve adjustments in other taxes or fundamental adjustments to the transfer system. Consequently, the state-level tax administrations are maintained. Compensation to "losing states" was provided; however, this was lump-sum and time-bound for 5 years from 2017. This arrangement did not involve a permanent realignment of the transfer mechanisms, as in the PRC, e.g., with the introduction of an equalization system for current transfers. The GST reforms have contributed to the significant growth performance and resilience in India.

Pakistan, on the other hand, reverted to the GOI 1935 colonial split, and assigned both the GST on services and its administration to provinces under the 18th Amendment (see below). Revenues remain moribund, growth has been weak, and the country has been skirting on debt default and reliance on a series of IMF programs that have provided a thin life line.

The GST integration, together with the use of a unique individual NID number, has formed the basis for rapid digital reforms in India. Ironically, the unique national NID number (with all the characteristics of a unique identifier) was introduced a decade earlier in Pakistan as part of the post 9/11 anti-money laundering and terrorism financing agenda, but the problematic tax policy and administration design has prevented any significant progress toward digital transformation of either the tax system or the economy, despite successive IFI-financed tax and administration reform programs (TARPs).

Toward an Agenda for Tax Reforms in Pakistan

There have been many **attempts to address poor tax design and administration in Pakistan**. An assessment in 1974,[29] headed by a former governor of the central bank, suggested that VAT should be considered to address corruption. This was followed by several IMF technical assistance missions. Analytic work by Ahmad and Stern (footnote 9) formed inputs to the National Taxation Reform Commission (NTRC) in 1985, drawing on the theory of reform to illustrate the need for a set of coordinated policy actions, taking into account the impact of tax policies on incentives facing firms and households in different circumstances; externalities, labor markets, and distributional considerations for both tax and investment decisions; and administrative costs.[30] The NTRC extrapolated these insights to also address corruption and smuggling, with the intention to take the tax/GDP ratio from 14% in the mid-1980s to 20% by 1990,

29 Government of Pakistan, March 1974, *Final Report of the Taxation Commission*. The commission was formed in 1970, before the separation of Bangladesh, and Alan Tait (later at the IMF) was a consultant.

30 Some of the analytic papers were published subsequently: E. Ahmad and N. Stern. 1986. Tax reform for Pakistan: Overview and effective taxes for 1975–76. *The Pakistan Development Review*. 25. pp. 43–72; E. Ahmad and N. Stern. 1990. Tax reform and shadow prices for Pakistan. *Oxford Economic Papers*. 42. pp. 135–159; and E. Ahmad and N. Stern. 1991. *Theory and Practice of Tax Reforms in Developing Countries*. Cambridge University Press.

while maintaining a focus on growth. Indeed, a 1986 assessment is noteworthy, in that this has been consistently ignored. In his cover note to the finance minister, the chairperson of the 1985 National Tax Reform Commission (Qamar ul Islam) described the Pakistan tax system:

> "...as stated in our letter dated 15 May 1986 transmitting our interim report, the three basic maladies from which Pakistan is suffering at present are tax evasion, smuggling and corruption. These are inter-related and one feeds on the other."[31]

The NTRC 1985 concluded that a coordinated approach is needed to reform all taxes and administration and that a ***tax-by-tax approach with tax administration determined separately would not do***. However, the next serious Pakistani report led by a former World Bank senior vice president focused separately on administration. The **2001 Shahid Husain Committee report was not wrong in recommending a modern functional approach to tax administration in Pakistan, with a strong focus on digital transformations**.[32] However, as predicted in the 1985/86 NTRC, without close linkage with the tax policy agenda, this reform would have minimal impact. Despite a world-class national NID number (unique, with check digits) established very effectively by the National Data Registration Authority following 9/11 (predating the Indian *Aadhaar* by almost a decade), the tax/GDP ratio continued to slide to around 10%, pushing the country into an increasingly vulnerable state.

In 2004, **a $130 million tax administration reform program financed by multilateral development banks (MDBs) was initiated with a significant component for computerization**. The original intention was to use the National Data Registration Authority NID number and generate a "data warehouse" that would streamline tax administration. Neither the Federal Board of Revenue (FBR) nor the panel of international advisors had a clue how this information integration would be achieved. Toward the end of the project in 2009, the tax administration had not produced a conceptual design for the computerization that clearly identified what would change and why and how the digitization would be used, and the tax/GDP ratio continued to stagnate at or below 10% of GDP. The tax system created impediments to doing business, and the "exemptions" handle provided political levers to authorities, and were quite profitable for the staff of the FBR. Departmental orders by the tax administration proliferated and clearly overrode the tax policy objectives of the budget process and bypassed Parliament. Attempts to remove exemptions in successive IMF and World Bank programs were partially successful and reversed as soon as the adjustment programs expired, as the underlying interests and disincentives remained unchanged,[33] leaving the tax/GDP ratio stranded at or below the 10% level (Figure 8).

31 Letter from Chairperson Qamar ul Islam to the Finance Minister, 31 December 1986.

32 Government of Pakistan, *Report of the Task Force on the Reform of Tax Administration*, Islamabad, 14 April 2001 (Shahid Husain Task Force). See also Government of Pakistan. 1985. *Report of the Tax Reforms Commission*, (Qamar ul Islam Commission), in which the tax administration was labeled as the most corrupt of Pakistani institutions.

33 World Bank. 2023. *World Bank Support for Domestic Resource Mobilization*. Independent Evaluation Group, World Bank.

Figure 8: Tax Performance in Pakistan

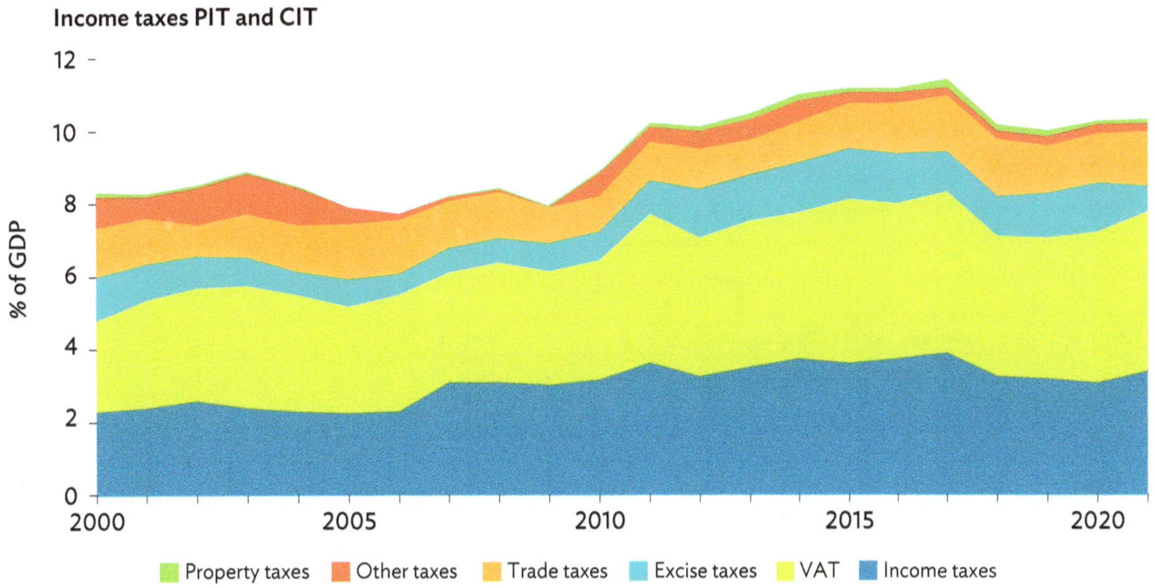

CIT = corporate income tax, PIT = personal income tax, VAT = value-added tax.
Source: OECD Revenue Statistics for Asia and the Pacific.

To the extent that the **computerization effort achieved anything, it was to digitize existing processes and procedures, create duplication and complexity for taxpayers,** and increase the need to interact with the tax officials. It was declared unsatisfactory by the World Bank in early 2008. The Income Tax Notification SRO 243/13 order by the FBR justified all past and future issuance of exemptions by the tax administration without reference to Parliament. However, another MDB-supported package for reforming the tax administrations of around $300 million (TARP-II) was designed in 2013, after the first TARP was deemed a failure, this time also including support for provincial tax administrations to implement the unworkable split GST on services.

A principal problem has been that, from the outset, the VAT has been implemented as a production excise, often fixing a "reference" sale price of the goods in question. This results in backward shifting of the incidence of the tax—and destroys the principle of taxes on inputs being offset against taxes on outputs. This also gives rise to the demand for exemptions. As entire segments of the economy become "exempt," it becomes even harder to determine the tax element in the goods, or determine appropriate export refunds, opening the way to rent-seeking behavior.

The 18th Amendment to the Constitution in 2010 reiterated the GOI 1935 split in tax bases, except that the GST on services was assigned to the provinces, along with the administration of the split GST. The VAT on services was difficult enough to administer at the central level in India, yet the 18th Amendment established new administrations at the provincial level for the split assignment of the GST. In reality, this has worked like a surcharge on imports and trade, or almost like the old "octroi" that was imposed on trading across local jurisdictions and that was abolished by the Musharraf regime. **The net effect has been, as expected, that the tax acts as an impediment to doing business**—the opposite of what the VAT/GST was designed to achieve.

Pakistan has received more technical assistance in tax policy and administration than most countries—including from the Fiscal Affairs Department of the IMF since 1990, and under the TARPs. Yet, the tax/GDP ratio has continued to decline—from around 14% in the mid-1980s, to around 12% in the 1990s, falling to below or around 10% since 2000. The geopolitical causes of the dependency on the IFIs and important bilateral donors are chronicled in Ahmad and Mohammed (2018), and the political economy aspects preventing major reforms are addressed in a recent monograph (Ahmad, 2024).

Figure 9 shows that **none of the main tax heads (income taxes, VAT, or even excises) come close to potential tax capacity** (see World Bank Tax Revenue Dashboard). As Pakistan lurches toward its 25th IMF program since the 1980s, its tax policy agenda is in disarray.

- There is a continued reluctance to address the politically sensitive GST issue, despite the mistaken split assignment. **A solution is to establish a unified tax administration for the GST, while keeping the constitutional assignment**.

Figure 9: Tax Capacity and Tax Performance in Pakistan

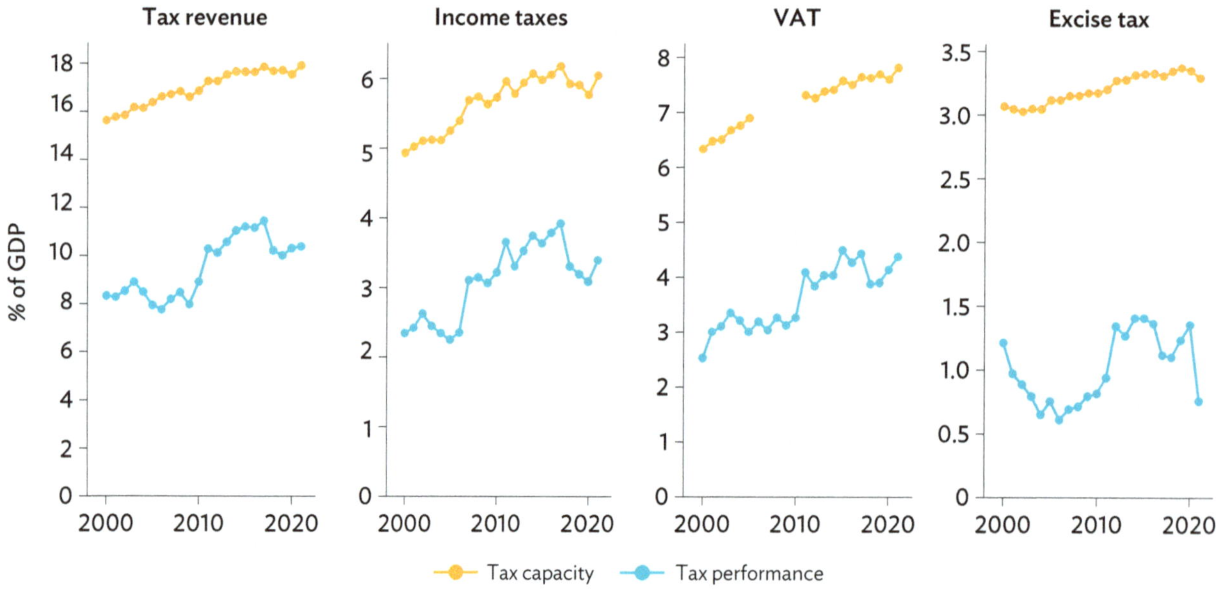

GDP = gross domestic product, VAT = value-added tax.
Source: World Bank Tax Revenue Dashboard.

- While the focus has turned to the income taxes for "equity purposes," with the GOI 1935 **split income tax base it is very hard to tax nonwage income,** especially emanating from agriculture. The income tax base is largely composed of formal-sector wage earners, with withholding at source (Figure 10). **Attempts to register more individuals under the PIT are not likely to raise much revenue in the medium term and are likely to be regressive**.

- With the proliferation of "infant industries"—many of which are over 70 years old—and "protected" sectors including loss-making state-owned enterprises, **the CIT also performs poorly both in terms of coverage and revenues generated** (Figure 10).

- **Attempts to determine property valuations by the FBR are misguided**. This reinforces the valuation–ownership model of property tax, but eliminates local decision-making that is essential for the "yardstick competition" needed for this model to work and to generate local accountability.

- A weak coalition government, unable to address serious structural imbalances in assignments and institutional arrangements, **is turning once again to SEZs as part of the solution for growth, and a digital expansion of the income tax base**. The SEZ income tax exemptions are likely to be offset by BEPS Pillar 2, whether or not Pakistan accedes to the BEPS treaty. As mentioned above in relation to Mexico, an effective coverage of the value chain by the VAT is needed to better integrate SEZs into the domestic linkages.

Figure 10: Personal and Corporate Income Taxpayers in Pakistan

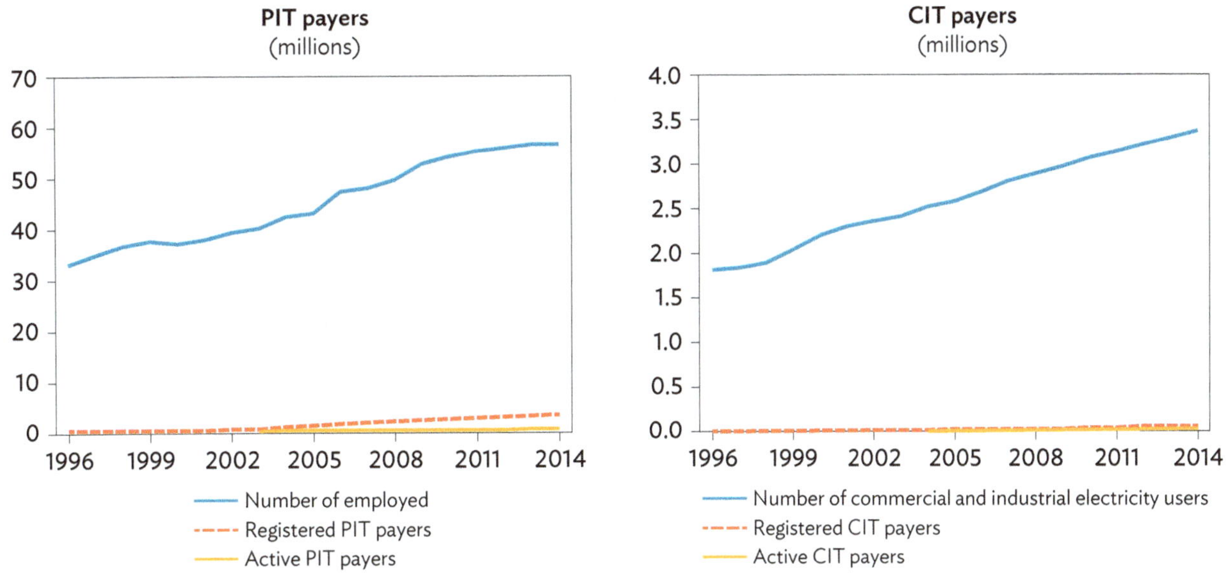

CIT = corporate income tax, PIT = personal income tax.
Source: S. Cevik. 2016. Unlocking Pakistan's Revenue Potential. *IMF Working Paper*.

- In the hope of using digital tools more effectively, **focus turned to e-filing and point-of-sale registers**. The problem is that, with *fixed taxes on small taxpayers, and a broken GST/VAT chain*, there is no incentive for small firms and retailers to join the system. Indeed, it provides yet another point of contact and possible rent-seeking opportunities for tax officials that the small taxpayers are keen to avoid. Following a mass campaign by the new administration in March 2024, only 50 retailers registered with the FBR by the mid-April deadline.[34]

In keeping with the advice of the Qamar ul Islam 1985 NTRC, given the history of failed tax reforms in Pakistan, and drawing on experiences of relevant countries, it should be possible to derive a set of coordinated multilevel tax policy and administrative reforms for the short-to-medium term. This may require a coordinated set of recommendations by the MDBs that could usefully be supported under the next IMF program under discussion.

Next Stages of the Indian Tax Reforms

The problems with the design of the GOI 1935 tax assignments were clearly in evidence as India pivoted to a more market orientation of fiscal policy. As shown by Ahmad and Stern (1984, 1987, 1991), the central government assignment of tariffs and excises affected a large number of intermediate sectors and not sales. This led to considerable "cascading," with unintended consequences. For instance, despite a public policy objective to not tax bicycles mainly used by the poorer groups, there was effective taxation negating the policy objective. The taxation of intermediate goods also led to distortions that considerably added to the cost of doing business.

Following the Gulf War in 1991, **India was affected by the disruptions to trade and remittances from the Gulf and had a balance of payments and debt crisis, forcing an IMF program**. Among a series of reforms set in motion in 1991 (Panagariya, 2004) was fiscal consolidation and converting the cascading excises and sales tax on services into a central government VAT. This was a first step to address the adverse effects of GOI 1935, while the assignment of revenues was not changed. The structural reforms initiated resulted in sustained growth and India has not had to go back to the IMF since then (unlike Pakistan). Despite the advantages of the move toward a split VAT at the center, it was clear that the system was inefficient and added to the costs of doing business.

34 S. Rana. 2024. Only 50 retailers register with FBR. *The Express Tribune*. 17 April.

Options to move toward an **integrated policy framework for the GST** (Empowered Committee of State Finance Ministers, 2009—see also Ahmad and Poddar, 2011)[35] led to a series of consultations resulting in a **constitutional amendment in 2016 to harmonize the GST**. Unlike in the PRC or Mexico, the Indian reforms did not utilize other permanent tax or transfer instruments in reaching a political settlement. However, losses by states with the new GST were compensated for a fixed period of 5 years using the additional GST revenues—leaving some recipient states in a difficult situation as the limited-period transfer ended. A GST Council, composed of Union and State Finance Ministers, determines policy decisions including the rate structures for the GST. This is efficient in the context of a split revenue base with integrated policy. However, in terms of subnational accountability and sustainable access to finance, **setting of rates by the GST Council turns an "own-source revenue" into effectively shared revenue**.

Unfortunately, the performance of **the Indian property tax remains poor after over a century of operation and considerable city-level experimentation** (0.25% of GDP and well below potential). However, the Indian property tax performs marginally better than the same tax in Pakistan, and some of the city experiments are promising as discussed below (Table 7).

As described in Ahmad and Brosio (2022), **the standard Indian property tax is based on the "ownership and valuation model" common in Western countries**. The valuation is based on an estimate of the annual rental or capital value of the property [Valuation (Metropolis) Act of 1869]. However, as pointed out in Bird and Rao (2012), the information base on the property tax in India is severely deficient and unreliable. This is partly because the cadaster is woefully out of date, and the valuation system has not kept pace with market price changes.

An alternative, tried in a number of Indian cities (e.g., Pune, Delhi, Bengaluru, and Surat), was to move to **a presumptive basis for taxing properties based on location and size to try to approximate true values**. The idea was to simplify and minimize the contact between the local tax administrators and taxpayers, and by an arms-length arrangement to minimize the opportunities for rent seeking and corruption. This reform was initiated in Patna in 1992/93 but failed to yield additional revenues. A similar outcome occurred in Delhi. However, in Bengaluru, the application of presumptive estimates led to a virtual doubling of the property tax revenues between 2007/08 and 2008/09 (Bird and Rao, 2012). The typical problems with arbitrary adjustments to presumptive measures have appeared recently in Bengaluru. *A 40% increase in valuations due to the new airport led to inequities within Bengaluru and had to be rescinded—and increases were capped at 25%.* Fine-tuning the valuations to specific neighborhoods, as well as a use of bands

35 The Empowered Committee of State Finance Ministers, November 2009, *First Discussion Paper on the Goods and Services Tax in India*; see also Thirteenth Finance Commission, *Report of the Task Force on the Goods and Services Tax*, December 2009. For a discussion see E. Ahmad and S. Poddar. 2011. GST Reforms and Intergovernmental Considerations in India. In M.G. Rao and M. Rakshit, eds. *Public Economics: Essays in Honour of Amaresh Bagchi.* Sage Press.

Table 7: Indian Property Tax Collections per Capita by City, 2015–2016
(₹)

	City	Property Tax Collection
1	Pune	2,676
2	Visakhapatnam	2,059
3	**Bengaluru**	**2,053**
4	**Hyderabad**	**1,686**
5	Chennai	1,224
6	Mumbai	1,121
7	Ahmedabad	804
8	Lucknow	714
9	**Delhi**	**705**
10	Bhopal	477
11	Thiruvananthapuram	469
12	Ludhiana	376
13	Raipur	311
14	Bhubaneshwar	256
15	**Patna**	**193**
16	Chandigarh	182
17	Dehradun	141
18	Ranchi	109
19	Kanpur	64
20	Jaipur	7

Note: Area-based implementation in red.
Source: Ahmad and Brosio (2022). Original sources: City Budget statement for financial year 2016 (FY2016) for all cities except Raipur; City Financial Statements for FY2016 for Raipur.

linked to the cost-of-service delivery, might yield more accurate changes and less political resistance. This would also enhance the effective accountability of the third tier of government that has been ensured legally with a constitutional amendment.

Recent attempts **to link components of the property tax to key public services through an earmarked "cess" move Bengaluru's property tax system toward a "beneficial model."** *This could circumvent the political economy constraint of fixed-income households in potentially expensive areas, and should be explored further* (see also the simulations for the PRC and Mexico).

With an area-location-based tax, the tax liability is determined through the application of a unit tariff (for example *n* dollars) to indicators or parameters of property size and value of use.[36]

[36] As described in Ahmad and Brosio (2022), the typical basic formula would be: *Tax due* = $n \times m^2$, where *n* is the unit tariff, let us say 10 euros, and m^2 is number of square meters.

Self-declaration of parameters by taxpayers, largely applied around the world for the main taxes, circumvents problems of information and administration capacity. It makes the area-based tax a viable solution for most emerging-market and developing countries. An area-based tax can be adapted to the local circumstances, and choosing the model according to the availability of information and capacity has a number of advantages:

- It can be implemented quickly with satellite technology, together with very simple verification and registration mechanisms.
- To the extent that it begins to tax high-end properties, this would be an improvement over the unimplementable ownership-valuation model that either misses out or undervalues high-end properties.
- Taxpayers' resistance would be addressed if the tax were linked to the provision of basic local services—enhancing accountability and meeting the SDGs more effectively.
- The tax can begin to use digital tokens (blockchain) to record transactions in real time and also simplify the contracting and registration process (Carstens and Nilekani, 2024 [footnote 6]; and see section VI). For the **digital transformation of the property sector to work effectively, it is important to also simplify the tax and fiscal arrangements**.

Together with the unique individual identifier number for 1.3 billion people (Aadhaar) and the introduction of digital payments systems (the Unified Payments Interface or UPI) (Figure 11), **the GST Constitutional Amendment spearheaded the digital transformation of the Indian economy,** making it competitive with countries like the PRC.

The shift from an origin-basis dual VAT **to a destination-basis coordinated GST has created a "level playing field" for firms and investors and reduced the cost of doing business**. It also has begun to address the missing trader problem and other forms of "evasion" also seen in Mexico.

The **information generation from the GST also provides tools for the taxation of the digital economy**. This will be helpful in laying the grounds for BEPS Pillar 1. The benefits regarding the CIT are also evident, as a buoyancy of 1.17 helps to offset the reduction in the rate of CIT maintaining revenues at 3.3% of GDP. The standard rate of 25% also means that India will have no problem with BEPS Pillar 2. The digital transformation also applies to the PIT, which is now almost paperless, with e-filing and a centralized database of 100 million taxpayers, generating 4.2% of GDP with a buoyancy of 1.5.

Figure 11: Fast Payment Systems in India and Brazil

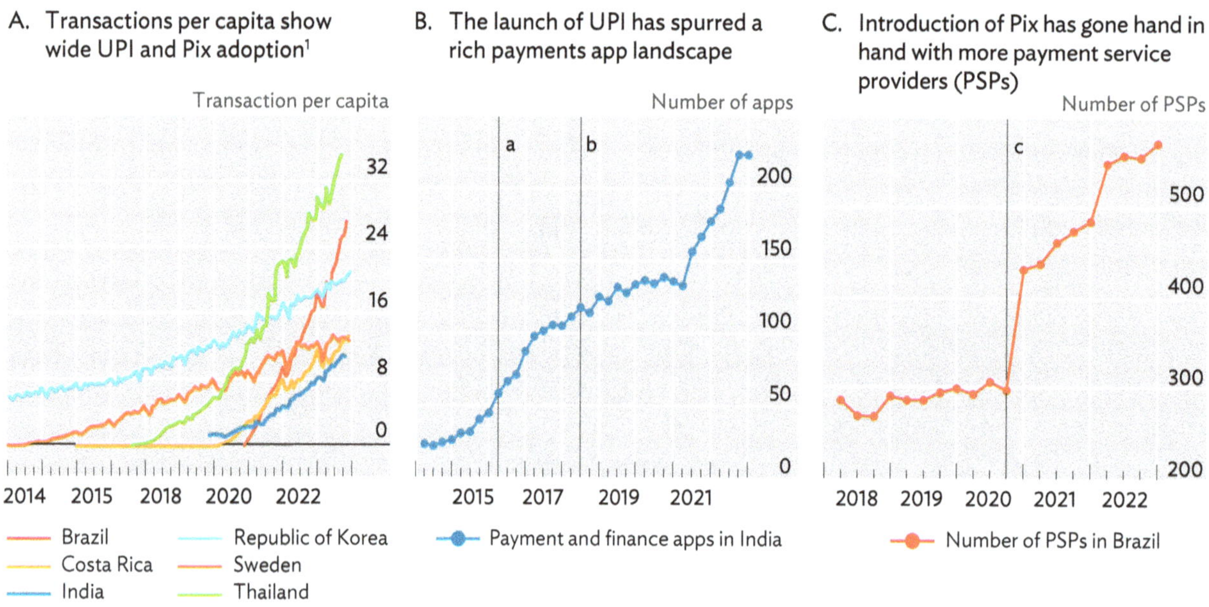

Note:
1 Monthly data.
a Introduction of UPI 1.0.
b Introduction of UPI 2.0.
c Introduction of Pix.
Sources: Central Bank of Brazil; World Bank; National Payments Corporation of India; Sensor Tower; Bank for International Settlements.

The tax reforms in India, led by the GST, resulted in a higher tax/GDP ratio (around 18% from 14% prior to the reforms—see first panel in Figure 12), anchored a **significant improvement in the business climate and a period of sustained growth,** and resulted in enhanced resilience. Thus, India was able to operate a more significant countercyclical fiscal policy to respond to the COVID-19 pandemic than Pakistan, and also manages a higher general government debt/GDP ratio (above the levels stipulated in the Maastricht-influenced Fiscal Responsibility Law) without risking a credit downgrade or debt distress.

Figure 12: India vs. Pakistan—General Government Tax-to-GDP, and Countercyclical Fiscal Response to COVID-19 Pandemic and General Government Debt

(a) General Government Tax-to-GDP

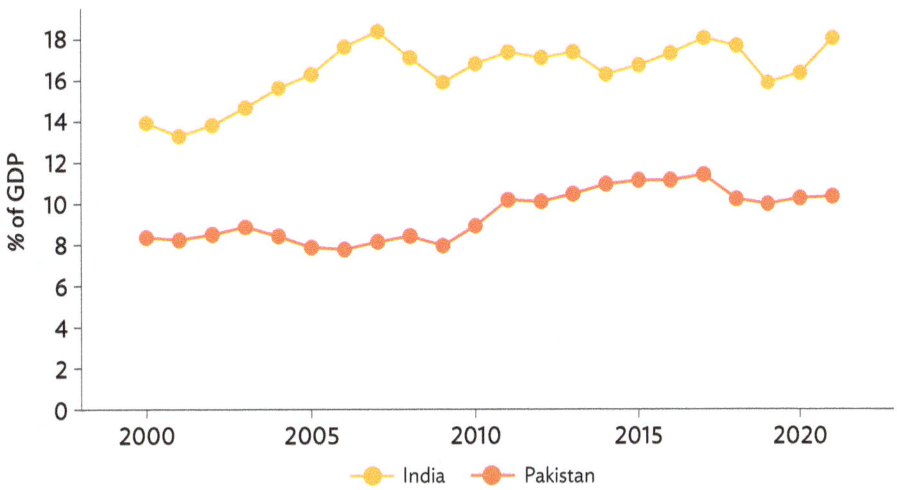

(b)

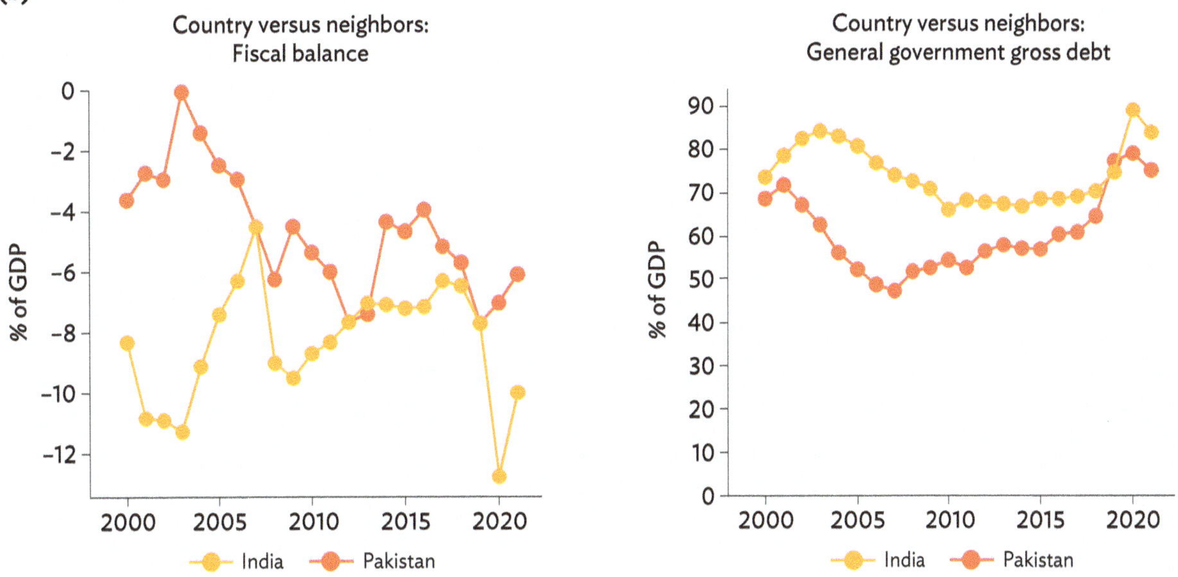

COVID-19 = coronavirus disease, GDP = gross domestic product.
Source: World Bank Tax Revenue Dashboard.

Unitary States in Asia

The Philippines

The Philippine tax system performs markedly below the levels achieved in East Asian countries (Chongvilaivan and Chooi, 2021; see also Figure 13). For specific taxes, the system performs well below its potential—especially for the VAT, but also the property tax (Figure 14) and below its own potential given poor design and tax expenditures (Ahmad et al., 2023).

The **Philippine tax system suffers from some of the same problems as in Pakistan, with exemptions and proliferation of SEZs for special interests, leading to segmented tax bases**. The Philippine tax/GDP ratio is higher than that in Pakistan, as it does not suffer from the political economy constraints of a federal arrangement. Given the difficult experience of dealing with the fallout from the Asian financial crisis in the 1990s, the Philippine authorities have been careful about not breaching prudential limits, even limiting the extent of the countercyclical fiscal easing during the COVID-19 pandemic.

Figure 13: Philippines—Tax-to-GDP Ratio in Relation to Thailand and East Asia

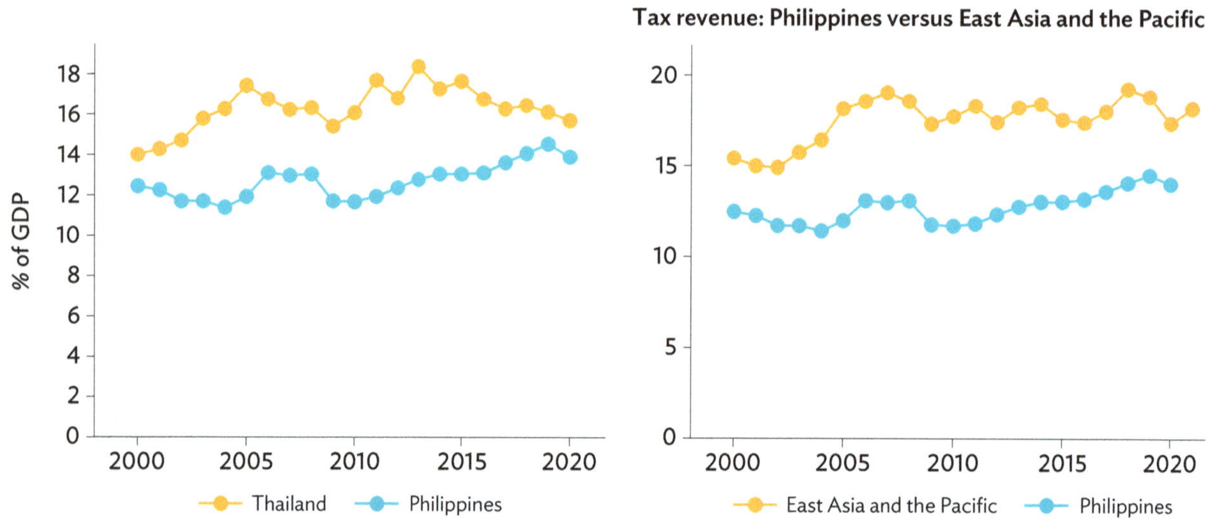

GDP = gross domestic product.
Source: World Bank Tax Revenue Dashboard.

Figure 14: Tax Capacity and Tax Performance in the Philippines

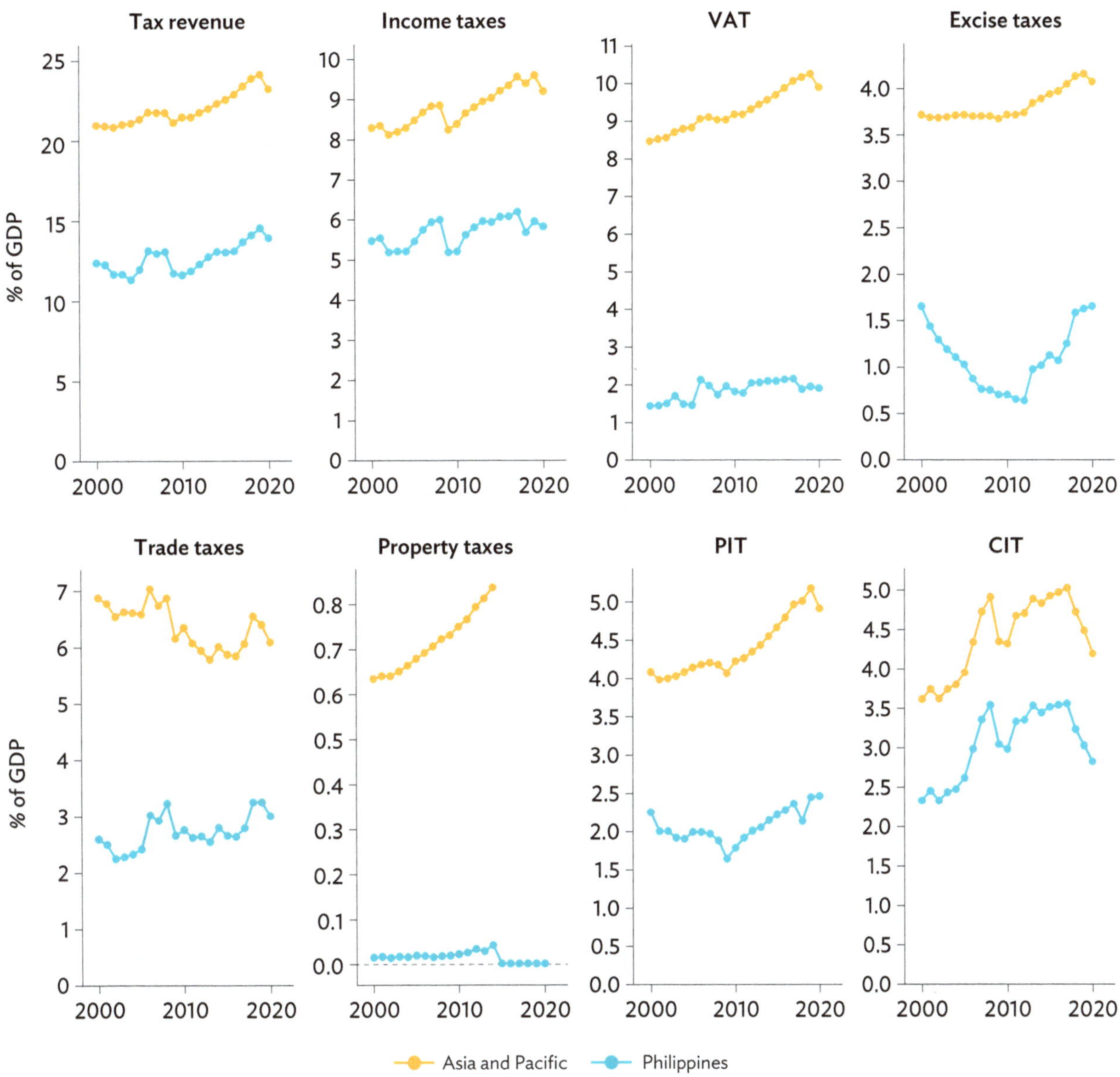

CIT = corporate income tax, GDP = gross domestic product, PIT = personal income tax, VAT = value-added tax.
Source: World Bank Tax Revenue Dashboard.

Ahmad et al. (2023)[37] identify three main problem areas in the Philippines:

- *VAT C-efficiency is among the lowest in the world*—at around 0.2, this contrasts with 0.8 achieved in other countries in the region. Extensive exemptions and domestic zero ratings vitiate the efficiency advantage of a VAT, as well as restricting the revenue potential. Closing the gap with other Asian countries would generate significant additional revenues (up to 4%–5% of GDP) and also improve the investment climate.

- *Philippine CIT rates are higher than other ASEAN countries,*[38] *but collections are among the lowest.* This leads to pressures for special treatments for all sorts of sectors. A more efficient strategy would be to bring rates into line with competing countries in East Asia and reducing the exemptions and special provisions.

- *The property tax is dysfunctional.* This paper develops proposals for a beneficial property tax for greater local accountability for the SDGs, and access to private finance for needed infrastructure. This should also assist in shifting activity away from metropolitan Manila, which must be at risk of disaster or inundation along with other coastal cities like Shanghai and Jakarta (C40 Cities, 2023).

The Bureau of Internal Revenue (BIR) has been significantly modernized according to international best practices but faces significant problems. As in the Pakistan case, attempts to move toward digital point-of-sale registers for large and export-oriented taxpayers are facing resistance as the efficiency gains depend crucially on full coverage of the value chain, including small taxpayers and micro, small, and medium-sized enterprises (MSMEs). The lump-sum taxation of MSMEs ensures backward shifting of the tax burden and reduces incentives for them to participate in a digital chain. Similarly, the extensive use of exemptions and SEZs reduces the ability of the BIR to function effectively, and also to adequately address the digital transformation of the tax system.

The digital transformation of the Philippine tax system will permit a better integration of taxpayers and types of taxes, as well as the design and operations of the BIR. Big data generation will permit the extension of the tax and benefit system to cover the informal sector and minimize leakages.

The Philippines has strengthened its regulatory frameworks for tax administration to institutionalize the BIR's digital transformation efforts. In January 2024, Republic Act No. 11976, known as the Ease of Paying Taxes Law, was enacted to simplify the Philippines' tax administration systems and encourage voluntary tax compliance. The law will enable electronic tax filing and return and harmonizes the VAT processes

37 E. Ahmad, A. Chongvilaivan and J. Lopez. 2023. *Fiscal Policy Options for Resilient and Sustainable Development for the Philippines.* Asian Development Bank.

38 The Corporate Recovery and Tax Incentives for Enterprises (CREATE) Act (Republic Act No. 11534) approved in April 2021 lowered the general CIT rates from 30% to 25%, and 20% for MSMEs.

to allow for e-invoicing and simplified VAT refunds. A dedicated tax office for MSMEs will also be established to provide more targeted services for this sector. Much will depend on how the full VAT base is integrated, to enable the Philippines to make best use of the BEPS agenda and ensure continuity of FDI.

The Philippines has signed the **BEPS agreement, and also wishes to better use the tax system to facilitate FDI and ensure resilience** and sustainable growth. Some of the key policy objectives and administration digitization goals are highlighted in Ahmad et al. (2023), reflecting some of the analysis and conclusions in this paper.

Thailand

Thailand has made significant gains in reforming the tax system, improving the business climate and attracting FDI, while also acceding to BEPS. Thailand is one of the countries to benefit from shifts in global trading patterns along with India, although not nearly as much as Mexico.

Domestic resource mobilization constitutes Thailand's fiscal strategy to support the government development programs and address long-term development challenges, including aging society and the rise in the digital economy. The Thailand Revenue Department (TRD) has made concerted efforts to modernize its tax administration system through digital transformation, resulting in a relatively high tax/GDP ratio at around 17% in 2014–2023.

The TRD established a digital transformation road map in 2021 to guide the transition to a fully digital tax system. By 2024, authorized service providers must be capable of preparing information and filing tax returns on behalf of taxpayers. Large companies will be mandated to create electronic tax invoices by 2025 and file tax returns electronically by 2027. The vision of the TRD digital transformation is for all entrepreneurs to be filing tax returns electronically by 2028. This phased approach provides clarity and a structured framework for the adoption of digital tax practices.

The move toward a digital tax system promises several advantages, most notably the new possibility of the TRD to utilize taxpayers' data. Another key benefit is the expedited processing of tax refunds. The TRD's objective is to reduce the processing time for VAT refunds from the current 15 days to a mere 3 days, a change expected to have a substantial positive impact on entrepreneurs and FDI. By embracing digital processes, business owners can expect faster and more efficient tax administration, allowing them to manage their taxes seamlessly from start to finish.

In September 2021, Thailand introduced the law on VAT on digital services as part of Thailand's post-pandemic fiscal consolidation strategy. The VAT on digital services is levied on foreign operators who receive a minimum of ฿1.8 million per year from providing digital services in Thailand. Foreign digital service providers must register online at the TRD website to submit their VAT filing and remit a monthly VAT payment. The process is available under a pay-only system without having to prepare tax invoices and input tax reports. The VAT on digital services is expected to generate over ฿5 billion in the first year and provide fair treatment for local digital service operators, which are subject to the existing VAT law.

With ADB support, Thailand commits to international tax standards under OECD/G20 Inclusive Framework on BEPS and the Global Forum on Transparency and Exchange of Information for Tax Purposes. In 2023, OECD's peer review of Thailand's legal and regulatory frameworks for transparency and exchange of information assessed the country to have a "largely compliant" rating, an improvement from the first peer review result in 2017. Likewise, substantial progress was made to strengthen domestic legal frameworks to implement the BEPS minimum standards in line with the OECD Two-Pillar Solution to base shifting and tax evasion.

Lao People's Democratic Republic

There was a huge increase the debt/GDP ratio in the Lao PDR during the COVID-19 crisis (Table 1), leading the country into debt distress. **This makes it imperative to improve the domestic resource mobilization performance that has been weak in the past decade.** Even before the COVID-19 pandemic, the average tax/GDP ratio in the country during 2010–2019 was 11.5%, significantly below the average for Asia and the Pacific (19.4%). Weak revenue performance has greatly contributed to the Lao PDR's limited fiscal capacity to spend on education, health, and social protection, and is seen as one of the root causes of rising public debt in the country.

The Lao PDR is pursuing determined fiscal strategies to ease macroeconomic vulnerabilities and support improvement in domestic resource mobilization (DRM) in the country. Moves toward digital transformation of the tax administration were initiated by the Tax Revenue Information System (or TaxRIS) in 2020 to process and manage taxpayer information, with the goals to enhance taxpayers' services and promote voluntary compliance. However, TaxRIS has not yet been fully developed for seamless online tax registration, filing, return, payment, and compliance management. Several basic building blocks remain to be addressed. Almost 70% of business units do not have business registration, and 87% do not have tax identification numbers (TIN).

The Lao PDR is enhancing the TaxRIS by using digital technology and expanding electronic services to reduce compliance costs and enhance transparency in tax administration. ADB has been assisting the Lao PDR authorities for TaxRIS enhancement by developing new tax administration functionalities in three ways. First, developing systems that allow taxpayers to register with the Tax Department, file returns, and pay tax liabilities online without physically going to the tax district offices can broaden the tax base through voluntary compliance. Second, effectively implementing an electronic invoicing system and administering accessible and convenient accounting systems for taxpayers to use will allow the Tax Department to monitor taxpayers' transactions and improve verification of tax refunds and declarations. Finally, leveraging new technologies, such as big data and blockchain, can provide the Tax Department with information to develop targeted enforcement programs and improve taxpayer services.

Taxation and Digital Transformation for Resilience in Small Island States

Small island states are particularly vulnerable to both climate-related shocks and trade disruptions. Resilience is enhanced through diversification of trade and productive capacity, prudent intertemporal management of assets, and strong DRM bases. Given the vulnerability to shocks, the UN SENDAI Framework for recovery and prevention of damage from shocks is important, and emphasized in Ahmad, Kattumuri, Lee-Emery (2023). In many small island developing states (SIDS), the climate challenges, as well as the havoc in the aftermath of the COVID-19 pandemic, provide important lessons. **The SENDAI Framework highlights the importance of local governments in ensuring basic services to the SDGs, but within a coordinated national and supranational arrangements.**

Many small island states have developed sovereign wealth funds (SWFs) to diversify against risk and vulnerability. Singapore, Kiribati, and Timor-Leste are all small island countries in the Asia and Pacific region and have SWFs. *The SWFs are an important element in establishing intertemporal resilience*, and ensuring that future generations (and governments) are not disadvantaged relevant to the current cohorts. However, excessive reliance on the SWFs can become an incentive to avoid taking difficult policy decisions and to "kick the can down the road." In such cases, the SWFs pose an impediment to the establishment of sound fiscal instruments and institutions, making such countries even more vulnerable to shocks.

Singapore stands out in terms of **its exceptionally well-managed SWFs and profitable Public Investment Fund**. Singapore's prudent fiscal management also led to the careful introduction of modern tax instruments, starting with the VAT, to replace colonial-era instruments that added to the cost of doing business and created productive distortions.

A key **objective of Singapore's tax reform was to better integrate with regional and global value chains,** and to become a center of excellence to attract higher value-added firms and to become a finance "hub." Singapore is also in the forefront of the digital transformation of fiscal institutions. All these structural measures enhance resilience.

Timor-Leste also benefited from a SWF, established with the assistance of the IMF following secession from Indonesia. However, the success of the Timor-Leste SWF has **hampered the development of DRM** instruments, despite recommendations from the Timor-Leste Fiscal Reforms Commission, and advice from development partners including ADB. Competition pressures, along with the burden of a dollar-based currency, have led to pressures to reduce existing tax rates that add to the cost of doing business, and this has increased the fragility of the public finances, and Timor-Leste remains far from resilient.

The contrasts between Singapore and Timor-Leste provide insights into the issues relating to resilience and tax policy instruments in small island states more generally. At the other end of the world, Jamaica's formidable fiscal strengthening over the past decade has helped establish the resilience seen during the COVID-19 crisis (Aslanalp, Eichengreen, Henry, 2024).

Singapore

Singapore is resilient and has **developed a diversified and advanced economy with significant digital transformation** of the economy and the fiscal system. It also has very **significant and well-managed SWFs**. The Government of Singapore Investment Corporation reported a net portfolio value of S$690 billion, and had a 20-year annualized real rate of return of 4.2% (this went up to 4.6% during 2022/23).[39] The returns for the Government of Singapore Investment Corporation are aimed to preserve and enhance the international purchasing power of Singapore's reserves. In parallel, at the end of the financial year on 31 March 2023, Temasek Holdings (owned by the Government of Singapore) reported a net portfolio of S$382 billion.[40] Despite a loss in 2023, Temasek has had a 9% 20-year return to the shareholder, with an average annual dividend of S$9 billion over the past decade.

39 Government of Singapore Investment Corporation 2022/23 Annual Report, 26 July 2023.

40 Temasek Review 2023.

A key element in the **resilience of Singapore has been the persistent effort to integrate with regional and global value chains**, and to establish the city state as a trading, production, and finance "hub." Reforming the cumbersome pre-independence tax system has been of high priority to make the country more "investment friendly."

In Singapore, the issue of a VAT was raised at independence in the late 1970s, but was not formalized until 1986. The Singapore Economic Reforms Committee was explicitly concerned about the *negative impact of high and distorting direct taxes on Singapore's competitive position and job creation prospects, and recommended a shift from direct taxes to the GST.*[41]

After extensive consultation, **a VAT was introduced in 1994 at a low rate of 3% with no exemptions, including for food, except for some finance services, and zero rating of exports**. This was accompanied by a reduction in the CIT and top PIT rate from 40%, removal of cascading excises, as well as reductions in the property tax. Compensation was provided for pensioners and spending on education was increased. The CIT was reduced gradually to 17%—the lowest in the Association of Southeast Asian Nations (ASEAN) region—and the simple but efficient VAT raised to 7%, and then to 9% in 2024 as part of the withdrawal of the post-COVID-19 countercyclical measures. By 2010, the taxation of goods and services generated 4.7% of GDP in Singapore (with a VAT rate of 7%), whereas in Pakistan, a country that had a head-start in introducing the GST, a 17% GST rate generated less than 3% of GDP around the same time (this contrasting case is discussed further below). Clearly, the extensive exemptions and preferences in the Pakistan GST explain some of the differences in performance.

Importantly, **the absence of exemptions in the Singapore VAT permits immediate and accurate refunds on exports, supporting the strong trading and export-oriented production structure**. It is worth noting that following the global financial crisis of 2008–2010, a number of European countries shifted from distortive direct taxation to the VAT. For instance, in Portugal, a shift to the VAT from taxes on payroll or capital constituted a "fiscal devaluation," as it led to a reduction in export costs with the fixed exchange rate within the euro area (de Mooij and Keen, 2012).

The overall tax/GDP ratio in Singapore is around 14%—or below the indicative IMF "tipping point" (Gaspar et al., 2016). However, this is not a constraint regarding effective provision of key public services. For instance, the proportional spending on education, at 22% of all outlays (general government), is among the highest in the world (Thailand is 20%, the Republic of Korea 15%, Chile 16%, the PRC 14%, and the US 15%).[42] The The Programme for International Student Assessment (PISA) ranking placed Singapore as the best-performing country in the world with respect to education

41 Republic of Singapore. 1986. *Report of the Economic Committee—New Directions.*

42 *Government Finance Statistics Yearbook*. IMF.

outcomes.[43] It is interesting that the world ranking in education is heavily dominated by Asian economies: (1) Singapore, (2) Japan, (4) Taipei,China, (6) PRC-Macau, China (7) Viet Nam, (8) PRC-Hong Kong, China, and (9) PRC (B–S–J–G). Estonia (3) and Finland (5) are the highest-ranking European economies. The US is way behind, in the middle of the reported PISA scores. The excellence in education has undoubtedly played a major role in the structural reforms and growth in the Asian region over the past couple of decades, and has been a major factor in enhancing diversification and resilience.

Both the tax policy framework and administrative structure are relevant in the context of governance to prevent tax avoidance, base erosion, or outright cheating. Singapore has the advantage of a strong taxpaying culture, buttressed by a simple tax system, with a CIT of 17% and a single rate VAT of 7% with minimal exemptions. As a response to the unwinding of the COVID-19 countercyclical response, the VAT rate was increased to 9% as of 2024. Singapore has one of the most efficient tax administrations with among the lowest collection costs in the Asian region at 0.088% of GDP (relative to, say, Japan at 0.148% of GDP, and Italy at 0.188).[44]

The simplicity in the tax policy framework, following the Tanzi dictum to avoid complexity, is a principal requisite for an efficient administration, and has permitted Singapore to be in the forefront of the transition to digital tax processes and procedures. This transformation has involved electronic transactions and data submission, along with simplifying tax law, policies, and processes, where possible. Again, the digital transformation has been led by the VAT.

Many, but not all elements, of the Singapore fiscal reform package are applicable to other emerging-market economies. Some of the general lessons from Singapore apply to most SIDS:

- A key feature of the Singapore reforms is the role of a properly designed **VAT in reducing the cost of doing business as well as improving competitive position**.
- Singapore is a small unitary state, with relatively good information on both the sources and uses of funds. Unlike many other larger Asian countries, Singapore is **not constrained by the need to balance the interests of subnational governments**. This avoids the problems with tax or transfer reforms that occur in unitary multilevel countries such as the PRC and Indonesia, as well as in federal states such as India and Pakistan.

[43] OECD. 2016. *PISA 2015 Result*, 6 December 2016. PRC is now represented by Beijing–Shanghai–Jiangsu–Guangdong (B–S–J–G).

[44] OECD Survey Responses, *Tax Administration Costs*; OECD Statistical Data Base; and Eurostat.

- The Singapore tax reforms in 1994 showed that **there is a need to think about the gainers and losers of any reforms**. Any set of tax reforms must involve an assessment of the effects on private producers and the country's competitive position, as well as the need to avoid or mitigate a negative impact on the poorest groups that are unable to participate in the labor market.

Timor-Leste

At independence, Timor-Leste had depleting petroleum reserves, virtually no fiscal institutions, and no central bank. It was therefore entirely **appropriate to establish an external SWF, or Petroleum Fund as it was called in Timor-Leste, with the assistance of the IMF, along with the use of the dollar**. As explained below, a fixed percentage of the returns was to be used for the budget to prevent premature depletion of the reserves.

The Timorese authorities have prudently managed limited natural resource revenues through the operations of the Petroleum Fund. **Budgetary spending is a function of the estimated sustainable income (ESI) that limits drawdowns from the Petroleum Fund to 3%.** The ESI is calculated as the level of withdrawals from the fund that would stabilize the net present value (NPV) of the assets of the fund.[45] This effectively protects the actual value of the fund. Actual annual withdrawals can be higher than 3% provided the government submits to Parliament a detailed explanation of why it is in the long-term interest of the country, and this has been resorted to in the recent past.

During periods of high oil prices, the ESI permitted the reduction in the rates of Timorese taxes (on income, customs, and sales). However, the ratcheting up of growth has accentuated the need to provide corresponding current spending, as well as operation and maintenance expenditures. Consequently, it has been increasingly difficult to limit withdrawals to ESI as the non-oil fiscal deficits have grown larger and required increasingly larger withdrawals from the Petroleum Fund and drawdowns of cash balances.

In addition to the volatile oil prices, the additional element governing the ESI is the rate of return on Petroleum Fund assets invested. **A prudent investment policy has been followed in the past,** with 65% of assets held in safe Treasuries and 35% in equities (Timor- Leste Petroleum Fund Annual Report, 2020). While the rate of return (1.39% in 2023)[46] has been lower than that which could have been earned if there had been

45 The ESI of the Petroleum Fund is based on an estimate of "petroleum wealth," which is estimated each year as the sum of the assets of the fund carried over from the preceding year and the NPV of future petroleum revenues. The calculation of NPV is based on prudent volume and price assumptions for petroleum and in practice, withdrawals are limited to 3% of the NPV of the fund assets.

46 Banco Central de Timor-Leste. 2023. *Quarterly Report of the Petroleum Fund of Timor-Leste, 30 June 2023.*

a larger investment in equities, this did not prevent losses. The fund recorded more than $2.5 billion losses during the first three quarters of 2023 due to weak investment returns and asset revaluations. Unless there are inflows from a new hydrocarbon field or considerable change in the government's fiscal policies, the Petroleum Fund balance is expected to be fully depleted by 2024 (World Bank Timor-Leste Report, December 2022, p. 44).

A number of commentators (e.g., Sachs, 2010) **questioned the wisdom of "locking up" resources in a Petroleum Fund managed abroad,** in the light of substantial domestic investment needs in physical and social infrastructure, for which the ESI limits may be inadequate. In fact, in a country with significant investment and social protection needs, it makes little welfare sense to focus exclusively on the "NPV of petroleum wealth" in foreign bank accounts—in a sense this involves a transfer from the current relatively poor generation to a future and possibly more prosperous generations to follow. Indeed, the future generations may be even better off as a result of prudent investment decisions *made* by the current generation—and this is the sense of the Sachs critique, which has much merit. Indeed, many versions of SWFs now explicitly permit investments in domestic infrastructure. For instance, the Indonesian Investment Authority, established in 2020,[47] is investing heavily in sustainable infrastructure transformation—e.g., electric vehicles and their ecosystem including nickel, and geothermal energy to help retire coal-fired plants. Despite investment needs in Timor-Leste, there is a danger of running down the Petroleum Fund balances as production at the Bayu-Undan fields has stopped. **A positive balance is desirable for insurance purposes including economic shocks, such as the COVID-19 pandemic and downturns in petroleum prices.**

However, something must replace the logic of the ESI, if Timor-Leste is not to face the risk of "wasting" the petroleum wealth, losing an insurance buffer, and becoming more vulnerable to the vagaries of an increasingly uncertain international environment. **Some form of a golden rule might be appropriate for the Timorese environment.** In a very simple formulation,[48] current spending could be restricted to non-oil revenues, and investment would be financed by prudent drawdowns from the Petroleum Fund and concessional borrowing.

Government revenue in Timor-Leste continues to be primarily derived from the offshore petroleum sector, with only a small proportion of taxes collected from the domestic (nonpetroleum) economy. Domestic resource mobilization, through further reform of the tax system, must be a key component of necessary fiscal reforms aimed at sustaining Timor-Leste's government finances over the longer-term. This is particularly important as petroleum revenue is now projected to decline steadily in coming years.

47 The Indonesian Investment Authority invested $1 billion in 2024 toward the green transition, and $2.1 billion since founding in 2021. The initial injection of $5 billion brought in $1.1 billion in foreign financing. At the end of 2023, it had $9.5 billion of assets under management.

48 E. Ahmad and R. Rabanal. 2010. *Timor-Leste: Tax Reforms to Enhance Investment Climate and Fiscal Sustainability*. ADB.

Given the need to attract FDI, a number of "distortive taxes" were reduced in the Tax and Duties Act of 2008, including the following:

- reduction of the marginal income tax rate for both business profits and individual wages from 30% to 10%;
- up-front deductibility (full depreciation) of business inputs; full and indefinite carry-forward of business losses;
- removal of the minimum income tax;
- import duties and sales taxes cut from 6% to 2.5%;
- service taxes lowered from 12% to 5%; and
- removal or simplification of excise taxes on particular items, among others.

Timor-Leste's direct tax system was brought in line with or below other Asian countries (Table 8). The CIT rate of 10% compared favorably with the average rate in six Southeast Asian countries of 26%.[49] This might need to be reviewed in light of BEPS Pillar 2.

The reforms also simplified tax procedures, resulting in some improvement in tax administration, but the ADB report[50] suggested further work was needed in preparation for a modern policy and administrative framework.

Table 8: Marginal Tax Rates (Highest Slab) in Southeast Asia, 2009
(%)

	Corporation Income Tax	Individual Income Tax
Timor-Leste	10	10
Indonesia	28	30
Malaysia	25	27
Philippines	30	32
Singapore	18	20
Thailand	30	37
Average	**26**	**30**

Source: Authors' calculation.

49 These countries are Indonesia, Malaysia, the Philippines, Singapore, Thailand, and Viet Nam.

50 Please refer to Ahmad and Rabanal, 2010.

The **private investment law provided tax holidays of various durations**. **These are redundant and unnecessary, and the overlapping of tax holidays and the 100% loss carry-forward contains disincentives for large investments**—as large investments during the tax holiday period would not carry forward to later years. This may be seen with a simple example. Assume that a large investment of $1 billion is made in year 1, and that the project earns $100 million per year. It would recoup the investment in 10 years during which the tax liability would be zero. With a tax holiday overriding the loss carry-forward, there would be a loss outstanding of $500 million at the end of the holiday, and this cannot be carried forward. In addition, there would be a tax liability of $50 million over the next 5 years, and the project investors will take longer to recoup their investment. The proposal could create incentives for the investor to leave after the tax holiday, or apply for a new one. In effect, the tax holiday is redundant at best, or less advantageous to the investor.

As pointed out in Ahmad and Rabanal (2010), customs and final-point sales taxes constituted impediments to investment and exports. **The tax reform agenda would replace existing distortionary taxes, such as the customs and sales tax, by a more efficient VAT**. This could then be projected as an efficiency-enhancing reform with little or no impact on domestic prices or on poor people, and a low rate of 3% or 5% could be held, say, for a period of 5 years or so—replicating the strategy followed in Singapore and Japan to start with a relatively low level to minimize adverse reactions. This would better help to make Timor-Leste more competitive, and integrate with ASEAN neighbors, as well as raising revenues for more effective service delivery. The ADB report suggested the following:

- A VAT of 5% could replace the customs duties and sales tax of 2.5%. This would lead to a ***drop in the tax element of imported goods***.[51]
- **Most of the revenue will still be collected at the ports**, as applying VAT to imports is allowed under World Trade Organization rules. This will facilitate administration.
- **Commodities and services with negative externalities, such as tobacco and alcohol**, as well as petroleum products, could be subject to increased excises in order to meet the revenue targets, as well as improving health, equity, and efficiency concerns. The increased excises on petroleum goods may be applied at the production stage as well as income taxes.

The distributional effects of a VAT introduction would depend on the price changes at the time the tax is introduced. In the case of imported goods, in principle, the replacement of the 6.25% tariff by a 5% creditable VAT would lead to a negative net price effect—hence there will be a one-off general reduction in the prices of imported and tradable goods. This is not tantamount to deflation, nor would an increase be tantamount to

[51] E. Ahmad and G. Brosio. 2010. A VAT in the UAE: Distributional Consequences and the Social Sectors. In E. Ahmad and A. Al-Faris, eds. *Fiscal Reforms in the Middle East: A VAT for the GCC*. Edward Elgar.

inflation—only a one-off adjustment in relative prices. As far as domestic non-tradables are concerned, subsistence and informal nature of the remaining activities would limit the effect of the VAT on those consuming such non-tradable goods and services—this is likely the case in most rural areas and for marginalized populations.

If a higher rate of the VAT is needed, say 10%, it would be necessary to estimate the effect of the tax and price changes on different groups of the population, and then design compensatory mechanisms. This work has not been undertaken at present. **It is still worth carrying out a full distributional impact of a 10% VAT, in order to fully inform policymakers and examine the mechanisms needed for compensatory measures.**

The key recommendations of the Ahmad and Rabanal (2010) mission were to initiate additional research on **possible implications of a VAT, determine the base and design issues, prepare the legal provisions, and initiate modernization of the tax administration to implement the reforms**.

Specifically:

- **Distributional impact**
    - There should be an examination of the impact of VAT on households in different circumstances. This will involve an empirical assessment based on recent household data.
- **Further specification of the VAT design**
    - This exercise would address the treatment of the finance and social sectors under a VAT.
    - The treatment of services and place of supply rules will need to be addressed.
    - The treatment of capital goods imports and production will need to be examined.
- **More detailed revenue modeling**
    - This would be based on options considered under the VAT design.
- **Inputs into the conceptual design for the tax administration reforms**
- **Preparation of the legal provisions**
- **Initiate a modernization of the tax administration.** As is also typically the recommendation from the IMF, the advent of a VAT provides a good basis for the establishment of a streamlined and efficient tax administration.

The ADB recommendations were taken up by the Fiscal Reforms Commission, that undertook joint work on tax policy design, including the distributional consequences of a VAT. In addition, the Commission commissioned drafting of a new VAT law, and initiated a major reform program for the tax administration. The distributional assessment is shown in Figure 15, and the proposed design of the VAT was shown to be progressive.

It is interesting that although Timor-Leste still does not have a VAT, it operated a VAT in the Bayu-Undan petroleum basin shared with Australia. The VAT in the petroleum sector **was not for revenue generation, but to provide offsets on VAT on inputs,** as virtually all of the petroleum is exported. The passing of the VAT law is required for the Sunrise Project, also shared with Australia for both revenue sharing and information. Although not standard IFI practice, the VAT on all purchases, including capital goods, with offsets or refunds as output is exported, **provides information on the quantum of transactions, production, and exports, and helps reduce possibilities of rent seeking**. This is particularly important when natural resource extraction and exports are managed by private firms under production-sharing contracts. This is also hugely important when there are centrifugal tendencies and potential conflicts.[52]

Figure 15: Impact of Value-Added Tax in Timor-Leste
(% of total household expenditure)

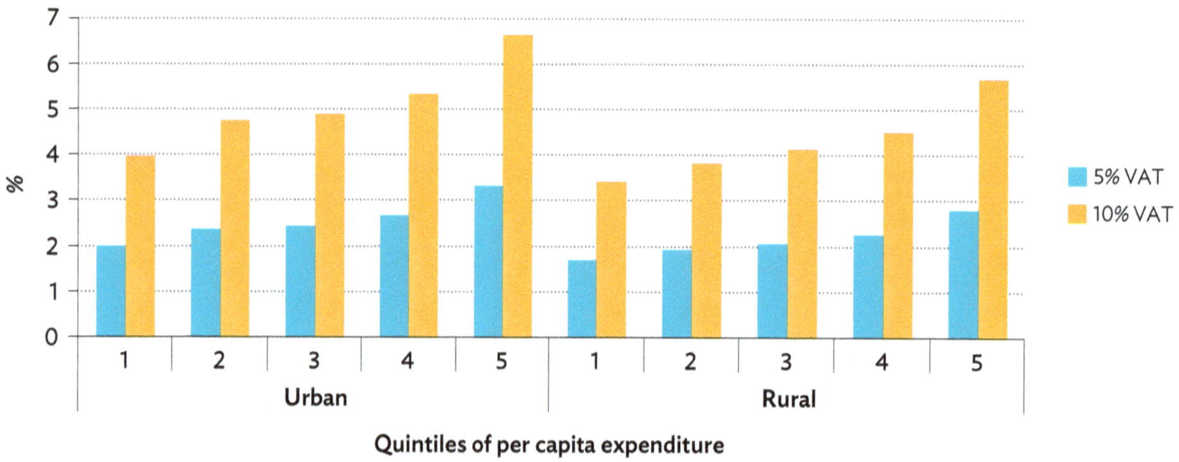

VAT = value-added tax.
Source: E. Ahmad and M. Breton. 2016. *A VAT for Timor-Leste: Some Policy and Design Considerations in the Presence of Informality*. ADB and Timor Leste Fiscal Reforms Commission.

52 See E. Ahmad and L. Larsen. 2021. *Equitable Management of Petroleum Resources for Conflict Resolution in Libya*. OECD and European Commission.

The "package of reforms" recommended by ADB and endorsed by the Fiscal Reforms Commission (including the policy and legal frameworks and revamping the administration) was ready for implementation, but was shelved with a change in government. The delay in reforming fiscal policies and institutions and the onset of the COVID-19 pandemic crisis has meant that the FDI, predicated on exemptions and tax holidays, has been slow to materialize. **Timorese public finances remain very vulnerable to shocks, as noted by more recent IMF Article IV reports.**

Section V

Toward a Digital and Sustainable Economy—The Role of Tax Policy and Administration

The **foundation of a sound digital transformation of the economy lies in a sound base of laws, especially tax and fiscal, regulations, rules, and business norms and institutions**. It is useful to keep an overall architecture in mind, as a rapidly evolving environment can either yield considerable benefits or leave countries behind in situations of potential turbulence in global trading systems, and climate-related shocks of increasing intensity and frequency. One such proposed architecture is proposed by the Bank for International Settlements (Figure 16), encompassing the finance, fiscal, and real sectors (Carstens and Nilekani, 2024).

Figure 16: High-Level Architecture of the Finternet

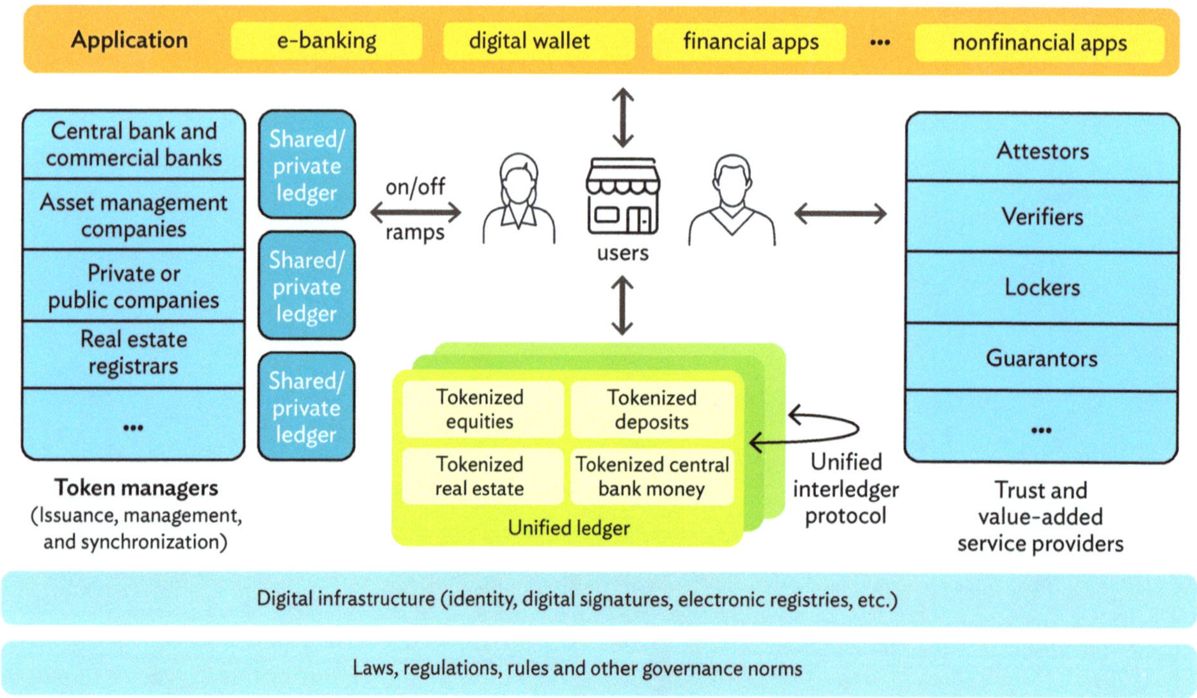

Source: A. Carstens and N. Nilekani. 2024. Finternet: the Financial System for the Future. *BIS Working Papers*. No. 1178.

A **huge simplification of processes and procedures is possible, and the case of asset transactions including for property is instructive**. The use of tokens and digital ledgers makes asset transactions and information generation instantaneous, cutting out tedious registration and recording procedures that plague many emerging-market countries (and some advanced countries). However, the advantages can be negated if the tax system remains cumbersome and essentially manual.

A key message of this paper is that it is important not to computerize existing processes and procedures as that is tantamount to "pouring concrete over a digital transformation agenda." (Gaute Solheim, Norwegian Tax Administration visiting the World Bank in 2023). Unfortunately, many computerization programs make precisely this mistake—e.g., in the failed attempt to require point-of-sale machines and e-filing in Pakistan. This despite having one of the key components in place—a digital system of individual identifier numbers. Unworkable tax policy and cumbersome administration just added to the cost of doing business, vitiating the advantages of a digital system. Three key issues stand out in the policy discussion above and which help to sequence some of the digital implementation questions in all cases:

- the VAT remains a key driver of the structural change;
- local own-source revenues are key to sustainable access to finance, and digital tokens and ledgers provide ways to bypass long standing difficulties; and
- the political economy of multilevel reforms requires a coordinated set of policy reforms and streamlined payment mechanisms—e.g., Brazilian Pix and Treasury Single Account (TSA)—but these elements are beyond the scope of this paper.

In this chapter, we first describe in greater detail some of the digital and institutional arrangements needed for digital transformations, and then highlight some of the policy options that could be considered in Asian countries—given the experience of unitary, federal, and small island states, and cross-fertilization options and experiences among developing countries.

Toward a New Tax Administration Paradigm with Digital Transformation and Local Autonomy

Digitizing the Tax Administration

A digital tax administration is all about efficient information generation and management, and this involves both policy and processes and procedures. As seen in the recent less-than-successful attempts to roll out point-of-sale machines that issue electronic invoices to small taxpayers and wholesalers, there is not much enthusiasm for this as long as these taxpayers are subject to "lump-sum taxation" and see no benefit to joining the scheme because the burden is shifted backward.

It is worth reiterating the **importance of not computerizing existing processes and procedures** without thinking through the architecture of a policy and institutional arrangement in a digital world. While considerable work is needed in this area before more specific recommendations can be drawn for individual countries, the following issues need to be kept in mind:

- **Use and management of big data and AI** can shift the determination of tax liabilities to an automatic basis from the audit-evading taxpayers, with a more arms-length role for the tax administration. ***It would also change the options for the design of tax administrations from the standard semi-manual tax administration model where the bulk of the work lies in verifying payments and reconciling accounts.*** Such activities and back-office staffing needs become redundant in a digital world.

- **Invoice matching** was not recommended in the typical structure and functions of an administration that relied on firms to maintain records and conduct (scarce skilled) audits. This led to the attendant focus on large taxpayers and increasing the registration threshold for VAT and income taxes. In turn, the resulting segmentation of the tax structure with incomplete information enhanced the ability and incentives to cheat.

- With big data, it is **much easier to integrate small businesses into the automatic invoice-matching system**—with detailed audits focused on very large and complex taxpayers, building on large-taxpayer units. This involves a potential shift in the role and functions of the tax administration to a more arms-length basis, with implications for tax policy and administration. The more efficient integration of small taxpayers is key to address informality and to stop cheating (by large taxpayers).

- **Simplification of procedures, reconciliation, and information by use of blockchain,** as well as management of returns and liabilities, would lead to an examination of the digital payments systems (tokens and digital registers) that interface with the Treasury or public finance management (PFM) systems.

- **Digital transformation permits easier exchanges of information** between domestic and foreign firms, facilitating FDI. This will transform the role of the tax administration, with most assessments carried out electronically and presented to taxpayers. An additional benefit is the exchange of information between tax administrations needed for a closer evaluation of transfer pricing, electronic services, and prevention of the cross-border leakage of revenues.

- **There is considerable potential for an integrated arms-length tax administration for all levels** of administration that sidesteps capacity constraints at the local level; however, the following are important:
  - **rate setting at the margin is critical**; and
  - there needs to be a **complementary equalization system** (administered within provinces or regions, or centrally).

Automatic transfer of funds to local accounts is essential, so PFM and TSA issues are also involved.

Tax Administration and Accountability

Tax and social policies need to align incentives facing different levels of government, firms, and households, and should remove possibilities of arbitrage or incentives to cheat. The policies, however, need to be supported by an administration that generates information, probability of detection, and effective sanctions to block the ability to cheat. Modern tax administrations are typically organized on a functional basis that focuses on reducing the compliance costs for taxpayers, minimizing direct contacts between tax officials and taxpayers (except in the taxpayer services and facilitation department), and relying on information generation and audit to identify anomalies and stop cheating. Rather than the outdated model of rewarding officials who bring in more revenues, arms-length institutions prevent direct contact between tax officials and taxpayers to ensure that revenues are collected efficiently, and cash flows tracked to prevent rent seeking and leakages.

A typical approach to subnational governance in many emerging-market economies, from Mexico to South Asia, **has been to establish separate tax administrations at different levels of government for split bases for the VAT and income taxes**. This leads to an increase in the complexity facing businesses. With the VAT, there are possibilities of arbitrage and "cheating" as the integrated flow of information becomes harder to achieve. The overall quality of the administration, especially for wide-area taxes such as the VAT and income tax, then is as good as the weakest link. The essence of local accountability, however, lies in the incentives generated by a control at the margin over rates and a specified base.[53] If a subnational government cannot control the marginal rate of a subnational tax, even with its own administration, the tax is no longer an own-source revenue but must be considered shared-revenue or transfer with relatively high collection costs (Ahmad, 2015).

53 See F. Ambrisanio and M. Bordignon. 2015. Normative and Positive Theories of Revenue Assignments. In E. Ahmad and G. Brosio, eds. *Handbook of Multilevel Finance*. Edward Elgar. There can be no hard budget constraints for subnational governments if they do not at the margin have control over the rates of a tax instrument that can be increased if the jurisdiction runs into difficulties in meeting its debt repayment obligations.

The typology of modern tax administration builds on a functional approach to administration that ensures arms-length operations (Figure 3, p. 29) by ensuring **that no single administrator can influence a tax payment, and that there are checks and balances based on the generation of information, risk assessment, and audit**. The enforcement function is particularly important as it reflects the collection of information from various taxes into a common database (e.g., VAT, CIT, and excises) that can be juxtaposed against real-sector variables and third-party information (e.g., asset holdings and consumption patterns) that provide a basis to signal risk-based audit. The outmoded approach to "incentivize" tax collectors by assigning bonuses in relation to taxes generated was needed in older systems of production-based excises (common in South Asia, for example) where the tax collector sat in a firm to monitor turnover. However, this was the source of great corruption and potential to "make deals" that are just not possible with the modern functional tax administration approach.

There is a continuum between policies and administration that ensures accountability. Shared revenues do not ensure accountability, as they do not represent control over tax rates at the margin. Hence, a shared tax cannot be used as an instrument to raise additional funds, should the need arise (e.g., as collateral for borrowing). Thus, in incentive terms, shared revenues are like transfers. The fact that there is subnational administration does not affect this assessment. For instance, even if all elements of tax administration were carried out at the state or provincial level, but the rates at the margin were determined in common with all jurisdictions, as is being the case with the GST in India, the subnational jurisdictions cannot claim the revenues as own source. In some cases, the state or provincial government could use the tax administration to influence the tax base, but that generates distortions and a possible "race to the bottom."[54]

The control over rate structures is much more effective in generating accountability, even if all or some elements of tax administration are managed at a different level of administration. Indeed, face-to-face negotiations between taxpayers and the tax administrator is a severe problem in the case of the property tax—e.g., in South Asia as well as Mexico, reflecting the problems in many emerging-market economies. The issue of the property tax is discussed further below.

By structuring the administration along functional lines, it becomes possible to concentrate on the key elements that make for an efficient tax structure. The flow and management of information is critical, both within a tax and across taxes. The registration function ensures that there is a common TIN for all taxes and levels of government—and facilitates the flow of information and linkages between different types of taxes, particularly VAT, income tax, and payroll tax. The enforcement function depends on a central database and flow of information across different criteria,

54 In Mexico, the race to the bottom occurred with the vehicle tax assigned to the states in 2010, because of cross-border competition and the possibility of accessing "gap-filling" central transfers to meet deficits at the end of the budget year (Piñeda et al., 2015).

particularly for VAT and income tax. This triggers flags for anomalies that need to be audited, with effective sanctions, as may be stipulated in the legislation. If the VAT and income tax bases are split, there is a danger that neither tax will perform effectively to raise revenues, while minimizing distortions and burdens on the taxpayers. With limited scope for local rate adjustments, there is even less justification to maintain or create multiple tax administrations, even though this tends to occur for political reasons, as in Pakistan following the 18th Amendment.

A local surcharge, generating the same amount of revenue as the revenue share, even with central administration, becomes an own-source revenue if the subnational jurisdiction has the right to raise or lower the marginal rate that it has been assigned. The surcharge or piggyback is typically not recommended in the case of VAT, but could work well with an integrated base for PIT. Note that the income tax base is split in both India and Pakistan, with multiple administrations, creating significant loopholes and rent-seeking opportunities. The surcharge on the *full income tax* could facilitate the integration of the tax administration, without loss of own-source revenue-raising powers, and be a way to block cheating in one of the fastest-growing revenue bases in emerging markets, as in India. Because the full tax base is used, cheating in income tax can be blocked with an appropriate use of information from the income tax—increasing the "total pie" available for the surcharge. Thus, higher revenues could be generated without a need to raise tax rates and further increase incentives to evade.

The surcharge approach is important in the context of a potential carbon tax that could form the basis for initiating structural changes, with the production and consumption patterns. Thus, the more congested and polluted metropolitan areas may require higher-than-standard carbon tax rates, without running the risk of the tax falling to zero in a race to the bottom (Ahmad and Stern, 2011). Again, the national tax administration capabilities would prevent the race to the bottom, while providing rate-setting options for provinces or states and potentially also municipal governments.

Modern tax administrations rely on effective management of big data. This involves the crossing of information from various sources to wages and employment, assets, profits, as well as production and sales. This points to a need to triangulate information from various sources, in order to detect potential mismatches and inconsistencies. Also, with increasingly decentralized records, such as blockchains, there has to be greater integration between the local and national databases, and between the tax administration and cash management functions. This is an increasingly important area for research, and a subject of great policy importance (Ahmad and Brosio, 2022).

A corollary of the integrated VAT reforms is that it generates information that can be used to stop the cheating and base shifting in the income taxes. This was examined in the context of fiscal reforms that draws on the Mexican 2013/14 experience, that provide an example of reforms designed to block cheating and informality.

While the targets for the SDGs, many of the basic services are delivered at the subnational level. Of the 17 SDGs, at least eight require actions at the local and regional levels: Nos. (3) health care; (4) education; (6) water and sanitation; (9) industry and infrastructure; (11) sustainable cities and communities; (13) climate action; (15) ecosystems, forests and desertification; and (16) reducing corruption. Apart from the direct delivery of the services, there is a need for investment in the supporting infrastructure. This typically requires a credible foundation of subnational own-source revenues that can be used to repay debt incurred for the needed investment in sustainable growth.

The implication is that more than the 18% of GDP identified under the SDG targets is likely to be needed over time. Many of the additional revenue options and tax bases must be concentrated at the subnational levels to ensure that subnational governance, investment, and borrowing decisions are soundly based. Unfortunately, this is where the institutional and governance preconditions are the weakest in emerging-market economies. This suggests the need for coordinated work to develop relevant policy and organizational alternatives suited to the appropriate context in specific countries. However, rules of thumb may be severely misleading.

The outcomes of the Mexican 2013 reforms exceeded expectations, and the revenue increase within 3 years compensated for the loss of petroleum revenues due to the decline in international oil prices. Despite the period of low growth affecting much of Latin America, largely due to the depressed prices for natural resources, particularly that of petroleum in the case of Mexico, the 2013 tax reform largely offset the fall in petroleum revenues, **raising an additional 4.2% of GDP** with no increase in the rates of the major tax instruments.[55] The exception was in the case of the carbon tax or excise that raised an additional 1.4% of GDP in 2016 relative to 2013. Although, during the period of depressed activity, the VAT increased by around 0.6% of GDP, the biggest gains were in *impuesto sobre renatas* (ISR) income tax that increased by 1.4% of GDP by 2016. These improvements helped maintain the level of public expenditures at precrisis levels.

A major part of the increase in revenues came from the very significant expansion in the number of registered taxpayers through the small taxpayer regime (Regimén Integrado Federativa) that required issuance of electronic invoices. This generated an extra 18.3 million taxpayers above the 2013 level of 38.5 million (Figure 10). This substantially closed the loopholes described in the preceding chapters. This suggests that a broader perspective on tax administration and tax policy is needed to achieve the most efficient results.

55 Mexican Ministry of Finance and Public Credit, Juan Rebolledo Márquez-Padilla, June 2017.

Policy Issues for Consideration by ADB Members

Context

It is striking that the promising digital transformations in unitary states (the PRC), federal states (India and Mexico), and small island states (Singapore) have all used VAT or GST as the instrument to initiate structural reforms. Digital transformations have generated a problem at the subnational level, as it is harder for more junior jurisdictions to set marginal rate structures to create own-source revenues that can be used as anchors for sustainable private financing (local government bonds, direct borrowing, and PPPs). Digital tokens and ledgers or blockchain operations provide a mechanism to bypass long-standing difficulties in property taxation in Asia (and elsewhere), and a comprehensive tax-transfer intergovernmental reform program is needed, even in small island states.

It is critical to design reforms to take account of gainers and losers, among levels of government as well as households. The reform to the transfer system in Mexico in 2007 as part of the IETU/ISR reform paved the way for the 2013 reform package that could then focus on fixing the taxes, and the interactions between the main taxes—particularly VAT and CIT. The offsetting transfer mechanism for the new tax system was also the basis for the 1993/94 reform package in the PRC.

One the most important lessons is to establish a complete VAT (with no major breaks in the value-added chain) to reduce the cost of doing business and to generate information to stop cheating in all major taxes, even if this may result in a slight overall loss of revenues, as was also the case in the PRC in 2016.

The tighter flow of information from the VAT also makes it harder for firms to cheat on their income taxes (the value added at each stage is the additional wages and profits generated). Thus, although the VAT revenue enhancement was positive in Mexico, the biggest benefit was in improved income tax collections. In order to achieve the tax-on-tax synergies, it is necessary to both achieve the full value-added chain (including a better integration with the small taxpayer regime that may use a simple cash-based accounting package, as provided by the State Administration of Taxation (SAT) in Mexico), but also the strengthening of functional capabilities of the tax administration to be able to match the information generated from different sources, together with a robust risk-based audit capability that would operate in common across many tax heads. While a special focus on large taxpayers may still be warranted, the integration of information from small taxpayers is critical to close loopholes, and has implications for the legal and de facto thresholds for VAT.

A tighter flow of information from the VAT can also help address the base-shifting problem associated with large multinational companies. The VAT, for instance, helps countries in the European common market to evaluate the extent of profits generated by corporations such as Google or Apple in the major European countries, and the extent of CIT avoided. For instance, the reductions in the CIT in the UK (to 20% currently and scheduled to go down to 17%) has not prevented Apple from paying virtually no tax in that country, and Google paying just 3% CIT over the past decade, counting penalties and negotiation. There is clearly scope for tightening the legal framework determining the CIT base to prevent such egregious avoidance, even in countries with efficient tax administrations.

Any special economic zone (SEZ) should be designed to maximize agglomeration effects and attract private investment, without exempting transactions from the VAT. The potential for leakage is particularly high, especially in countries with relatively weak tax and budgetary management systems. The main objective of creating a special zone or "hub" is to provide synergies between public investment and services to ensure uninterrupted supply of electricity, water supply, sewerage systems, as well as education and health facilities to "attract" private investment (both foreign and domestic) to benefit from agglomeration effects, locational advantages, and skilled labor. Tightening of corporate tax rules because of the "base shifting" phenomenon is an advantage, as this ensures that production actually takes place in these "hubs," and that they are more than vehicles for firms to "show profits," as in Ireland or Panama. The VAT is then critical as an informational and control mechanism in SEZs, and will not be expected to raise revenues, as much of the output from SEZs would be exported and subject to zero rating for VAT purposes. This consideration would again modify the traditional approach to the VAT in SEZs, which exempts all activities in those zones. Indeed, completion of the VAT chain makes the whole country a SEZ. For instance, the new international airport in Querétaro has led to a major influx of investment (Aerospace, Nissan, and BMW headquarters), thereby illustrating that infrastructure development (a new airport to complement the existing motorway links to CDMX and the US), a clean city environment and absence of congestion, and a university with skilled workers, are critical ingredients in making new "hubs" functional and well integrated with the rest of the economy.

The control mechanism associated with the information generated by VAT is also an important tool to monitor investment and production in the natural resource sector, including petroleum. This requires a modification of the typical recommendation made by the IFIs in relation to VAT, which permits VAT on capital goods to be refunded more or less immediately. Unfortunately, this removes the lever to extract information. The leakages from the Nigerian petroleum sector, documented by the Ribadu Commission Report,[56] could be plugged by utilizing all possible sources of information, of which the VAT is an important component. The more appropriate

56 Report of the Petroleum Revenue Special Task Force, 2012. *Report of the Petroleum Revenue Special Task Force* (Chairman, Professor Ribadu).

formulation, especially in countries with high levels of informality, may well be what is practiced in the PRC—to permit the VAT on capital and other inputs to be offset against VAT liability on outputs, or zero-rated when exports are verified. Of course, as correctly recommended by Professor Ribadu, it is also important to track the flow of funds, including the interface between the management systems of the petroleum company and the government's Integrated Financial Information Management System as well as that with the TSA.

While the overall distributional effects will depend on combinations of taxes and social policies, a careful design of the VAT itself will minimize the need for compensatory measures. For instance, excluding nonprocessed basic staples (wheat, rice, and maize) in different countries would go a long way toward "protecting the poor"—as argued by Ahmad and Stern (1991) in the context of India and Pakistan. This was also the approach taken by Mexico in its 2013 reforms—as the intergovernmental implications were minimal due to reform to the transfer system in 2007:

- Empirical work in Timor-Leste suggests that if the authorities were to implement a VAT which exempts nonprocessed food (rice, maize, and cassava), a single rate VAT would still be quite progressive (Ahmad and Breton, 2016; see also Ahmad and Stern, 1991).

- The Mexican experience shows also that it is not always appropriate to utilize conditional cash transfers (CCTs), such as the former *Oportunidades* program, to accompany tax reforms, such as the VAT or energy price reforms, including the introduction of a carbon tax. CCTs may be justified as stand-alone programs to support the poorest groups in society, usually in rural areas as in Pakistan[57] or Mexico, but the major concern is typically for poor and fixed-income workers in urban areas.

- The Mexican example further shows that the opposition to tax reforms in multilevel countries comes from powerful interest groups as well as lower-level governments that might be affected by changes in assignments or transfer and revenue-sharing arrangements. This is why the proposed adjustment in *Oportunidades* in 2010 to facilitate the VAT reform was rejected. In 2013, the VAT was reformed and a carbon tax simultaneously introduced, and the CCT was not utilized.

- The only compensation together with the package of tax reforms in 2013 was the minimum basic pension. However, that did not create labor market distortions or generate a "poverty trap." Indeed, energy price adjustments, as proposed in Indonesia, are likely to create the fiscal space for efficiency and equity enhancing health care coverage.

57 The Benazir Income Support Program in Pakistan was modeled on Mexico's now-defunct *Oportunidades* program, and largely targets poor rural households. It was implemented in 2010 with the support of the World Bank and bilateral donors such as United States Agency for International Development (USAID) and Department for International Development (DFID) of the UK, to support a VAT reform, which has been effectively abandoned.

A carbon tax, and excises more generally, need to eliminate "implicit subsidies" and prevent a "race to the bottom." There are two components in the Mexican or Indonesian context. The implicit subsidy argument suggests that the carbon tax should be imposed above a reference price such as the world price for, say, petroleum products. This ensures that there is no implicit subsidy, and it generates positive revenues as well as incentives for firms and households to adjust the choice of techniques and consumption away from environmentally damaging products. The piggyback on a carbon tax provides local flexibility to implement a higher-than-national rate, if needed, and also makes the tax an own-source of revenue that could be leveraged to access credit.

Multilevel issues are important in most tax reforms. There is a case for a higher carbon tax in the more congested parts of metropolitan areas, such as Mexico City or Jakarta, than in remote cities. However, assigning own-source taxes to states—such as the vehicle tax, *tenencía*, given the system of "gap-filling" transfers—has not had a very successful track record, as discussed above. Consequently, a piggyback on a central base and administration would be indicated to prevent a "race to the bottom." This also provides an own source of revenue for sustainable access to credit and financing of infrastructure. Similar issues apply with respect to "excises" meant to counteract health hazards, particularly with respect to the traditional "bads," such as tobacco and alcohol. However, in Mexico, there has been a sharp increase in obesity and diabetes, leading to an increase in health expenditure. While national taxes on sodas and confectionary are appropriate, and were introduced in the 2013 reforms, there may be a case also for higher taxes in the metropolitan areas where the consumption of such "bads" is greater. This brings us to the multilevel issues relating to governance that are critical, whether the focus is on federal countries like Mexico, India, and Pakistan, or unitary states such as the PRC and Indonesia.

Tax and spending issues need to be considered together. In East Asia, aging of populations is putting pressures on health budgets. Health-care costs are significantly influenced by access to clean water and sanitation. These are typically local functions, whether financed from local funds or earmarked transfers. In both cases, accountability at the local level is critical—and this involves both full information on spending as well as appropriate incentives for local governance. This links the spending directly to the presence of own-source revenues at the local level (Ahmad and Brosio, 2022). This issue is taken up in further detail in the next subsection.

Elements of a Tax Policy Agenda for Sustainable Growth in Asian Countries

The design and management of national and state or provincial taxes in many Asian countries could be improved in several respects. Some of the reforms would be facilitated by the planned digital transformation, and others depend on a political economy linkage with other taxes or intergovernmental transfers and should be considered as part of a coordinated "package."

Digital transformation could be initiated with the following:

- reform of an integrated VAT and administration for all BTB transactions, even if special arrangements are needed to bring in the small taxpayers;
- use of digital recording of asset transactions, including also the property tax sector; and
- better integration with the digital payments systems, such as UPI or Pix.

Some detailed issues arise that could form the basis of MDB discussions with Asian countries.

VAT and digital transformation

A modern and simple VAT with minimal exemptions not only generates significant **revenues** but also helps with creating **a level and integrated economic space, reduces the cost of doing business, and generates information** that facilitates the broadening of the income tax base and **reduces "leakages" and "cheating."** As seen in the PRC and Mexico, VAT introduction and reforms generate gainers and losers among provinces or states, ***and political economy considerations require the use of a "package of taxes and transfers" to offset likely resistance to the reforms.***

Digital transformations depend crucially on generation of timely and verified information that simplify both tax and spending design as well as institutional arrangements, policies, and procedures. Thus, to anchor a digital transformation, the VAT will involve the following:

- **Full information for digital transformation with coverage of business-to-business (BTB) value chain and the components of wages and profits** at each stage, requires integration of SMEs into the VAT value chain. This will require both policy and administrative reforms along with digital transformations.
- **Removal of exemptions and special provisions to encourage investments or distribution for BTB transactions.** This applies to a significant portion of the tax base, leading in Pakistan and the Philippines to some of the lowest C-efficiency estimates in the whole world (OECD, 2022).
    - **Exemptions in the VAT are tantamount to "input taxation"** that prevent input tax offsets being carried further in the value chain. Hence this introduces "cascading," which the VAT was invented to eliminate, adds to the cost of doing business, and discourages exports.

- **Exemptions in a VAT lead to breaks in the information chain** that prevent the use of information from the VAT for other taxes, making it easier to avoid income tax liabilities. **An integrated VAT has the potential to stem "cheating" in the income taxes and** hiding of transactions and value added (wages and profits), including by large taxpayers.

- **VAT can be applied to mining and drilling** and would force the disclosure of activity levels, including with production-sharing contracts, even if the activities are mainly for export.

- **VAT that covers the full value chain and facilitates immediate export refunds or credit could also transform SEZ design and operations, which could better leverage domestic linkages.**

- **A critical element in the digital transition is to ensure that** the TIN is consistent with the National Identity Card (NIC). A **revised TIN or NIC needs to be mandatory for any public transactions,** especially customs, but also other public activities such as contracts and procurement, and registration of labor or companies.

With an integrated **VAT and complete coverage of the BTB value chain** (with C-efficiency rising from 0.2 to above 0.8 in Pakistan or the Philippines, or levels achieved in the PRC), there should be a significant enhancement in the tax/GDP ratio taking it toward sustainable levels and forming the main element in enhancing DRM resilience targets. This would also help create a level playing field and ensure that countries can take full advantage of greater global efforts to harmonize corporate taxation (BEPS Pillar 2, in particular).

- **Sequencing of measures for a "package of reforms" including VAT and tax administration**

  - **In the short run,** an integrated VAT in some countries might require agreement between the center and the states or provinces for a single administration, perhaps with a board of directors representing all federating entities. Revenues could continue to be distributed according to the constitutional arrangements in different countries. To facilitate tax-on-tax linkages, the new administration should also administer an integrated income tax and allocate revenues according to current laws.

  - **In the longer run,** a constitutional amendment might be needed in some cases (e.g., Pakistan) to reassign revenue functions, taking account of the efficiency and revenue gains of digital transformations, along with new own-source provincial revenues for accountability. A new fiscal equalization component would also be needed to avoid exacerbating spatial imbalances.

Political economy of distributional and environmental concerns

Distributional and environmental concerns should be met through taxes such as the income tax or excises on goods consumed primarily by rich people. While it is not appropriate to integrate distributional concerns into a VAT, excluding nonprocessed foods from the VAT goes a long way in protecting poor people without jeopardizing the flow of information from the full value chain (as was the compromise in the 2013/14 Mexican reforms).

Political economy considerations influence environmental taxation, such as a carbon tax. Much more is needed than just tagging "green taxes," such as an excise on petroleum products. Given that petroleum is an intermediate good, the "effective" equivalent of the tax in the prices of related goods needs to be incorporated into the reform program.

Reforms and just transitions should be based on a broad perspective on gainers and losers, especially in countries such as Pakistan and the Philippines with lower-than-average per capita emissions in relation to other Asian countries as well as the global average. Yet, *appropriate carbon pricing is needed to tax the rich* users of energy and petroleum, and to *reduce pollution and congestion especially in large metropolitan areas in each case, regardless of the extent of cross-border pollution*. This can be achieved through a piggyback or local surcharge on the **petroleum levy**[58] that would be higher in Karachi or Manila than in remote and less densely populated regions. This would reduce migration and informality and help **shift investment and employment** to CCCs and SEZs with domestic linkages.

More precise estimates for **distributional or environmental concerns** could be based **on a system of additional petroleum excises**. These would require systems of demand and supply estimates using household and production data—see Ahmad and Stern (1991) for method and examples from South Asia, Ahmad and Viscarra (2016) for Chile, and Ahmad and Viscarra (2021) for Mexico. While static microsimulation estimates, often used by the IFIs to establish gainers and losers in policy reforms, are a useful starting point, **a full assessment would also incorporate the impact on employment generation and the environment, that also lead to improvements in health and living conditions**.

58 This was originally called the "petroleum tax" but was changed to "petroleum levy" to avoid having to share the revenues with provinces.

The following options would be relevant across many Asian countries:

- **Excises on carbon, emissions; taxing "bads"** (e.g., plastics, cigarettes, and alcohol)—the suggested relative rate structures would depend on the effective taxes (including indirect effects on other sectors and products—see the discussion on India); inequality aversion of the policymakers; and weights on human, social, and natural capital.

- **Local piggybacks or surcharges** (e.g., on excises for health externalities and environmental damage) would provide significant additional revenues and also appropriate (dis)incentives in more polluted or congested areas. A higher piggyback in Karachi or Lahore, than in CCCs and SEZs, would generate incentives that support the spatial transformation for sustainable growth.

Local or subnational tax administrations are not needed for surcharges or piggybacks, and subnational autonomy and accountability depend on the ability to set piggyback rates at the margin.

CIT, BEPS, and redesigned SEZs

In a rapidly globalizing world and **especially strengthened competition from neighboring South and Southeast Asian countries, there is a case for reducing the standard rate of the CIT to bring the rate structure in line with the regional standard, especially since some of these countries are competing for FDI**. Revenues would be protected by rationalizing CIT exemptions and preferences, and making better use of BEPS, especially Pillar 2.

- **Setting minimum CIT rates with BEPS would effectively establish a minimum tax on profits, even if generated in a SEZ, or in a country that has not signed on to the global treaty.** It would make no sense for Pakistan to subsidize the finance ministries of investor source countries.

    - Consideration should be given to **shifting to full loss carry-forward rather than exemptions to tax the effective profits over the life cycle** of the investments. This would reduce the incentives to cheat. It would also eliminate a bias in favor of short-duration projects.

- **SEZs should concentrate on agglomeration effects and better linkages with the domestic economy.** Implementing the VAT in SEZs would enhance domestic linkages, increasing the attractiveness of Pakistan for FDI, provided there is immediate and full refunds or credits for exports. This would depend critically on the planned digital enhancements of the Federal Board of Revenue (FBR) and procedures that directly credit the accounts of the relevant taxpayers.

PIT and tax-on-tax linkages

In most emerging-market countries, PIT coverage is often driven by formal-sector wages. Nonwage income, including from the very extensive informal sector, agriculture, and assets, is typically difficult to capture with traditional tax administration methods. The options expand as the economy develops and digital transformation takes hold, especially with a fuller coverage of the value-added base. The latter provides information on wages and profits (components of value added) at each stage, as is important in expanding the base of the income taxes.

- **PIT enhancements depend on the effective use of big data, and full coverage of BTB value added by the VAT is a huge advantage.**

- **A critical precondition for the improvement in information flows is NIC-TIN linkage.** This is a cornerstone of the digital transformation and needs to be examined carefully.

- **Generating information from blockchain on finance and real asset sales** will assist in expanding the base significantly beyond taxing formal-sector wages.

Subnational Issues

Perhaps the weakest common denominator in the Asian context is the establishment of an own-source revenue system at the state, provincial, and local levels. This is needed to induce subnational accountability, and also ensure sustainable access to private finance—a key objective of the sustainable growth agenda. Both simplification of the policy framework and administrative arrangements (that do not have to be at the subnational level) would assist with the move toward digital transformation that is likely to create a completely new opportunity set.

Own-source revenues, where the subnational jurisdiction sets the rate at the margin (including within a band in unitary states), are essential for accountability. This is particularly important in countries that have devolved spending to the subnational level. Thus, subnational administrations should institute the following:

- It is important to **align incentives of subnational jurisdictions or local governments and the national tax administration** by permitting a piggyback on an integrated national PIT base. This would also encourage subnational governments to provide information that is more readily available to them, especially third-party data on living standards. However, the more developed cities, where rich people live, would likely benefit disproportionately.

- **A full reform that addresses political equalization and spatial equity concerns would involve a fiscal equalization system** in which a subnational piggyback on the income tax (and property taxes—see below) should be a factor determining standard revenue capacities, and hence the amount of transfers received.

- **The piggyback would also count as own-source revenue for subnational access to local government bonds or other access to private finance.** Shared revenues are not under the control of a subnational jurisdiction and are thus not appropriate in determining local borrowing or capacity to service liabilities.

Tax-benefit linkages and political economy of local taxation

A huge area of concern is the absence of effective own-source revenues at the local level in most Asian countries, given a dysfunctional property tax and a major push to devolve spending. While higher revenue shares are needed given the large vertical imbalance in each country, these do not ensure accountable use of revenues or appropriate decisions concerning financing the SDGs or associated investment design.

The potential piggybacks on national taxes provide a convenient tax handle that can be implemented quickly, can unlock bond issuance as well as private finance, and do not require a new local tax administration. **Three other elements would help in overcoming a potential "race to the bottom"**:

- the piggyback could be **subject to a floor**;

- access to private funds and **borrowing could be made subject to generation of own-source revenues**, including the piggyback; and

- the fiscal equalization could include a **standardized estimate of what the jurisdiction should raise from the own-source taxes, that would be taken into consideration in the determination of the equalization transfer**. This, however, applies to all local own-source taxes and not just the piggybacked arrangements.

Property taxes are visible, "onerous," and generate political opposition, as Alfred Marshall noted in the 1890s. This seems to have been borne out in most emerging-market countries, and Pakistan is one of the worst examples in this regard, with negligible collections. Marshall correctly pointed to the importance of linking a simple property tax to basic services to overcome political resistance and turn an onerous tax into a beneficial one (Ahmad and Brosio, 2022).

Three distinct cases apply with respect to urban property taxes:

a. **Recurrent tax on noncommercial properties.** This provides the bulk of property tax revenues in most countries and is the most difficult to address largely because of a potentially "onerous" character of the tax. A major obstacle in emerging-market countries, from the PRC to Colombia to India, has been the political economy constraint of income-constrained households living in potentially expensive areas.

b. **Recurrent tax on commercial properties.** The political economy constraints faced under Case A do not apply, and there are far more transactions than for noncommercial properties. It would be appropriate to continue to apply the traditional market-based valuation–ownership model.

c. **Property sales.** All property sales, whether for commercial or noncommercial properties, should be taxed at the prevailing market price. Such sales can be taxed at both central and local levels and would benefit greatly from the digital transformation that is underway in many countries.

The ongoing work to establish property values by central tax administrations in a number of Asian countries can be used to establish relativities in a simple area-based system of bands, based on location and size. Accountability would be achieved with simple establishment of rates by the local authorities for the recurrent taxation of noncommercial properties. This has considerable potential (e.g., up to about 2% of GDP in the PRC, or a bit lower in Mexico). It is possible to pilot some of the "Marshallian" linkage with local service delivery. However, for commercial properties and all property sales, it is important to apply the accurate market rate, and a blockchain system can go a long way in establishing this. A significant area of work remains to be done in Pakistan on local taxation, urban transitions, and achievement of the SDGs and greater accountability and resilience. Some key points as follow:

a. **Use existing work on national valuation to establish rankings** for "potential bands" for an area–location-based recurrent property tax on noncommercial properties and use satellite technology (national tax administration) with low-tech local verification.

b. **Use of blockchain for all property sales at market values** would become a key element in the capital gains tax and provide information on assets for the proper working of income taxes.

c. **Market valuation for recurrent taxation of commercial and business properties is important** as more regular markets exist and also more robust information generation. Central government or FBR determination of property values is not appropriate in this context.

d. **An effective "fiscal equalization system" at each level of government is an essential complement to this reform.**

Taxation of agricultural land

Size, location, and irrigation status could also be used to revamp agricultural taxation linking to local public services for accountability purposes—see proposals for Pakistan outlined in Ahmad and Stern (1991). The **Ahmad-Stern simulation of acreage-based land tax for Pakistan was linked to a percentage of gross output (7.5%)** above a generous exemption limit of 12.5 acres of operational units (also graded by Produce Index Units) for insurance purposes. The exemption leads to an **increasing marginal tax rate for larger holdings, so is equitable,** and would have generated around 1% of GDP or more revenue than **the total provincial revenues at the time or federal development grants to provinces**. The crucial link with local public services—health care, basic education, and social protection for the locally identified needy—is needed for political acceptability and could **transform rural local governments toward better accountability and social service delivery**.

References

Ahmad, E. 2008. Tax Reforms and the Sequencing of Intergovernmental Reforms in China: Preconditions for a Xiaokang Society. In S. Wang and L. Jiwei, eds. *Fiscal Reforms in China*. Oxford University Press.

Ahmad, E. 2015. Governance and Institutions. In E. Ahmad and G. Brosio, eds. *Handbook of Multilevel Finance*. Edward Elgar.

Ahmad, E. 2018. Rebalancing in China—Fiscal Policies for Sustainable Growth. *Singapore Economic Review*. 63 (4). pp. 861–884.

Ahmad, E. 2021. Multilevel financing of Sustainable Development in China: Options for Inclusive, Resilient and Green Growth. *Journal of Infrastructure and Policy Development*. 5 (1). p. 1251.

Ahmad, E. 2021. National and Subnational Tax Reforms to Address Informality. In C. Deléchat and L. Medina, eds. *The Global Informal Workforce*. International Monetary Fund.

Ahmad, E. 2024. *Political Economy of Tax and Digital Transformations in Pakistan*. PIDE monograph.

Ahmad, E., J.L. Añorve, and H. Viscarra. 2021. *Productivity Enhancement and Sustainable Employment in Mexico: Building Forward Better from the Pandemic and Creating Inclusive Growth*. ILO ACT/EMP.

Ahmad, E. and M. Breton. 2016. *A VAT for Timor-Leste: Some Policy and Design Considerations in the Presence of Informality*. ADB and Timor-Leste Fiscal Reforms Commission.

Ahmad, E. and G. Brosio, forthcoming. Towards a "Third Generation" Approach to Fiscal Federalism. In R. Bahl, ed. *Festschrift for Jorge Martinez-Vazquez*.

Ahmad, E. and G. Brosio. 2006. *Handbook of Fiscal Federalism*. Edward Elgar.

Ahmad, E. and G. Brosio. 2015. *Handbook of Multilevel Finance*. Edward Elgar.

Ahmad, E. and G. Brosio. 2022. *Beneficial Property Taxation for Emerging Market Countries—Financing Sustainable Development and Post Pandemic Recovery*. Palgrave Macmillan.

Ahmad, E. and G. Brosio. 2022. Financing Sustainable Local Spending and Infrastructure in China. In E. Ahmad and G. Brosio, eds. *Beneficial Property Taxation for Emerging Market Countries*. Palgrave Macmillan.

Ahmad, E. and N. Stern. 1984. The Theory of Reform and Indian Indirect Taxes. *Journal of Public Economics*. 23. pp. 259–298.

Ahmad, E. and N. Stern. 1987. Alternative sources of government revenue: illustrations from India. In D. Newbery and N. Stern, eds. *The Theory of Taxation for Developing Countries*. Oxford University Press for the World Bank.

Ahmad, E. and N. Stern. 1991. *Theory and Practice of Tax Reforms for Developing Countries*. Cambridge University Press.

Ahmad, E., R. Kattumuri and A. Lee-Emery. 2023. *Fiscal Policy Options for Resilient and Sustainable Development*. Commonwealth Secretariat.

Ahmad, E. and A. Mohammed. 2018. Pakistan, the US and Bretton Woods Institutions: A Continuing Great Game (with A. Mohammed). In A. Pande, ed. *Routledge Handbook of Contemporary Pakistan*. Routledge.

Ahmad, E. and N. Stern. 2011. Effective Carbon Taxation and Public Policy Action. In M.G. Rao and M. Rakshit, eds. *Public Economics: Essays in Honor of Amaresh Bagchi*. Sage.

Ahmad, E. and S. Poddar. 2011. GST reforms and Intergovernmental Considerations in India (with Satya Poddar). In M.G. Rao and M. Rakshit, eds. *Public Economics: Essays in Honor of Amaresh Bagchi*. Sage Press.

Ahmad, E., G. Brosio, M. Garcia-Escribano, J.A. Gonzalez Anaya, and E. Revilla. 2007. Why Focus on Spending Needs Factors? The Political Economy of Fiscal Transfer Reforms in Mexico. *IMF Working Paper*. 07/252.

Ahmad, E., G. Brosio, and C. Pöschl. 2015. Local Property Taxes and Benefits in Developing Countries—Overcoming Political Resistance? In E. Ahmad and G. Brosio, eds. *Handbook of Multilevel Finance*. Edward Elgar.

Ahmad, E., I. Neuweg, N. Stern, and C. Xie. 2021. Policies for Structural Reform in PRC: Domestic Rebalancing for Strong, Sustainable and Inclusive Growth Within and Beyond PRC. In J. Svejnar and J.Y. Lin, eds. *China and the World Economy*. Edward Elgar.

Ahmad, E., J. Rydge, and N. Stern. 2013. *Structural Change Leads to Tax Reforms Leads to Structural Change*. LSE Asia Research Center and China Development Forum.

Ahmad, E., M. Niu, L. Wang, and M. Wang. 2020. *Designing Beneficial Property Taxation for Sustainable Development in China—Evidence From Six Cities, Including Guangzhou*. LSE Program on Financing Sustainable Urban Transitions in China and Mexico.

Ambrosanio, F. and M. Bordignon. 2015. Positive and Normative Theories of Revenue Assignments. In E. Ahmad and G. Brosio, eds. *Handbook of Multilevel Finance*. Edward Elgar.

Aslanalp, S., B. Eichengreen, and P.B. Henry. 2024. Sustained Debt Reduction: The Jamaica Exception. *Brookings Papers on Economic Activity*.

Bahl, R. and S. Wallace. 2008. *Reforming the Property Tax. A New Approach*. Andrew Young School of Public Policy.

Bird, R. and G. Rao. 2012. *Coping with Change: The Need to Restructure Urban Governance and Finance in India*. Institute on Municipal Finance and Governance.

Brockmeyer, A., H. Kleven, J. Spinnewijn, and M. Waseem. 2015. Production versus Revenue Efficiency with LimitedTax Capacity: Theory and Evidence from Pakistan. *Journal of Political Economy*. 123 (6). pp. 1311–1355.

Carstens, A. and N. Nilekani. 2024. Finternet: the Financial System for the Future. *BIS Working Papers*. No. 1178.

Chongvilaivan, A. and A. Chooi. 2021. *A Comprehensive Assessment of Tax Capacity in Southeast Asia*. ADB.

de Mooij, R.A. and M. Keen. 2012. Fiscal Devaluation and Fiscal Consolidation: The VAT in Troubled Times. *Working Paper*. 12/85. Fiscal Affairs Department, IMF.

Drèze, J. and N. Stern. 1987. Theory of cost-benefit analysis. In J. Auerbach and M. Feldstein, eds. *Handbook of Public Economics*. Vol 2. North Holland.

Eichengreen, B., P. Gupta, and A. Ahmed. 2003. *India's Debt Dilemma*. NCAER.

Gao, Q. 1995. Problems in Chinese intragovernmental fiscal relations, tax-sharing and future reforms. In E. Ahmad et al., eds. *Reforming China's Public Finances*. IMF.

Gaspar, V., L. Jaramillo, and P. Wingender. 2016. Tax Capacity and Growth: Is There a Tipping Point? *IMF Working Paper*. 2016/234.

Gil Diaz, F. 1987. Some Lessons From Mexico's Tax Reform. In D.M.G. Newbery and N. Stern, eds. *The Theory of Taxation for Developing Countries*. Oxford University Press for the World Bank. pp. 333–360.

Hinrichs, H. 1955. *A General Theory of Tax Structure Change during Economic Development*. Harvard University Press.

Kanbur, R. and M. Keen. 2015. *Reducing informality. Finance and Development*. 52. pp. 53–54.

Keen, M. and J. Mintz. 2004. The Optimal Threshold for a Value-Added Tax. *Journal of Public Economics*. 88 (3–4). pp. 559–576.

Kuhn, T. 1970. *The Structure of Scientific Revolutions*. International Encyclopedia of Unified Science, University of Chicago Press.

Kumar, D. 1982. The Fiscal System. In D. Kumar and M. Desai, eds. *Cambridge Economic History of India*. Vol II 1757–1970. Cambridge University Press.

Levy, S. 2008. *Good Intentions, Bad Outcomes: Social Policy, Informality and Economic Growth in Mexico*. Brookings Institution Press.

Luo, X. and N. Zhu. 2020. *Migration, Agglomeration and Regional Structural Transformation in China*. LSE Program on Financing Sustainable Transitions in China and Mexico.

OECD. 2022. *OECD Revenue Statistics in Asia and the Pacific 2022*.

Panagariya, A. 2004. India in the 1980s and 1990s: A Triumph of Reforms. *IMF Working Papers*. WP/04/43.

Rodrik, D. 2024. *Addressing challenges of a new era. Economics—How Should it Change?* Finance and Development. IMF.

Shi, Y.B. 1995. Unifying the Enterprise Income Tax and Reforming Profit Distribution Between Government and State-owned Enterprises. In E. Ahmad et al., eds. *Reforming China's Public Finances*. IMF.

Tanzi, V. 1987. Quantitative Characteristics of the Tax Systems of Developing Countries. In D. Newbery and N. Stern, eds. *The Theory of Taxation for Developing Countries*. Oxford University Press for the World Bank.

Tanzi, V. 2023. *Monitoring the State or the Market: From Lassez Faire to Market Fundamentalism*. Cambridge University Press.

Wang, W., A. Wu and F. Ye. 2018. Land use reforms: Towards sustainable development in China. In Ahmad, Niu and Xiao, eds. *Fiscal Policies for Sustainable Development in China—Rebalancing in Guangdong*. Springer.

www.ingramcontent.com/pod-product-compliance
Lightning Source LLC
Chambersburg PA
CBHW041756220926
51847CB00014B/221
* 9 7 8 9 2 9 2 7 0 9 2 3 5 *